MW00772058

Provide for the Common Defence

Border Defence

Christopher Hatley

Strategic Planning Press

Provide for the Common Defence

Strategic Planning Press

For further information, please contact:
cnhatley@earthlink.net

Printed in the United States of America

Provide for the Common Defence
Christopher Hatley

1. Title 2. Author 3. Political Science/U.S. Government

Library of Congress Control Number: 2008905142

ISBN-10: 0-9817214-0-0
ISBN-13: 978-0-9817214-0-8

For my mother, Annie Josephine Hatley,
who always was an avid reader.

Table of Contents

PART I
CURRENT SITUATION

Chapter One

Reconnaissance

No good decision was ever made in a swivel chair.
—General George S. Patton, Jr.

Patton understood this important fact: A leader needs to be on the ground, at the front, talking to the soldiers in the trenches and observing the battle first-hand.

I, too, understand this and though I didn't intend to become a leader, per se, in the United States' open-border crisis, whenever the topic came up, I found myself remembering the general's words. I knew that the lack of effective security along our borders was a problem; I knew that someone should be doing something about it—and that maybe, that someone should be me. But what could I do? I didn't even have all the facts, didn't really know what was going on along the front lines—the U.S.-Mexico border—on a daily basis.

The answer was clear: I had to be on the ground. And so in August 2006, and again in 2008, I spent several days along the border, where many of our U. S. Border Patrol agents are in the trenches.

Why did—why *does*—this matter so much to me? Because I'm a seventh-generation Texan, born and raised in Dallas by conservative parents who taught my three brothers and me to love our country and not to tolerate dishonesty. We are proud of the fact that our family's forebears came to Texas and fought in the war for the State's independence. And, like virtually every Texan going back to the mid-nineteenth century, and even as far back as the days of the Republic, our family has always understood the need for security against Mexican bandits, hostile Indians and outlaws.

Now, I'd like to make two points before I go further. First, the U.S. Border Patrol are a dedicated group of men and women, and I sincerely appreciate their candor and the work that they are doing for all of us. I can't say that enough. Second, to maintain their anonymity, I will not use the names of the Border Patrol agents with whom I spoke; nor will I reveal the locations of these interviews. Many agents are concerned about reprisals.

That fact alone illustrates the huge leadership void that exists in many levels of government. Too many people within the government, it appears, are beholden to big-money lobbyists and too busy "big dealing" to look out for the best interests of their constituents. It's true that some politicians tend to vote the right way—just often enough to stay out of trouble with the folks back home. However, they show no real leadership on the critical issues, such as our nation's growing problems stemming from our failure to secure our southern border with Mexico.

And that's a large part of the problem: The leaders are not out there on the ground. What's so hard about going to talk with the men and women of the U.S. Border Patrol, the soldiers on the front line? And I don't mean giving them the standard "VIP briefing" in the field. I mean hearing what they have to say, really listening to their concerns and then doing something about the issue based on that information.

When I first set out on my expedition to the border, my concept was to follow a plan of action similar to the methodology I followed as the inspector general (IG) at Fort Polk, Louisiana. There had been no intent to play "I gotcha!" during my watch as IG. The only objective I'd ever pursued was gathering the facts, regardless of where they led me.

Solely with that same interest in mind, I went to the U.S.-Mexico border with an inspection plan in hand, complete with a tentative time line, routes to the various port-of-entry border towns; objectives for each fact-finding opportunity; a set methodology for observing both U.S. and Mexican border communities; and specific questions to ask law enforcement and Border Patrol personnel. I was confident that my IG experience would facilitate my assessment of the general situation along our border with Mexico.

Starting out on the U.S. side of the border, I made some interesting observations. As is my practice while traveling, I stopped in a number of fast-food places to get coffee along the way and as I approached the border area, it was interesting to see how many cars in the parking lots displayed Mexican tags—it wasn't as many as I'd thought it would be. In fact, the majority of cars had U.S. plates.

Now, the interesting thing here is that although I estimated that fewer than two percent of all patrons in these fast food establishments were non-Hispanic, and even though most of the cars in the lots were American, virtually all of the language I heard being spoken inside was Spanish. Often, my conversation with an employee was the only one I heard that was *not* in Spanish. And I was still in the United States.

My next step was to drive through the U.S. border communities to see what I could find. As I did this, I saw countless Spanish bumper stickers, but no Mexican flags hanging on any of the houses. However, in one town with a population of over 33,000, I saw only two American flags hanging out.

At one point, I happened upon an elementary school that was letting students out at the end of the day. Children, parents and teachers walked around and out of at least 200 people, I saw only one woman who appeared not to be of Latino descent.

In another town, I stopped to ask people on the street for directions to the border-crossing point and to my surprise, most of them could not understand me. Keep in mind that I was still in the United States, and I was speaking English. I finally managed to find the crossing point, but I received no help from the local population—because we could not understand each other.

The next part of my procedure was to enter Mexico several times, at various places along the border from Texas to California, to observe operations at the ports of entry into the U.S. and see what was going on in the Mexican towns. At each port, there were several signs in both English and Spanish—and I'll grant that this is one instance where bilingual signs are necessary and helpful, since many people going back and forth speak only one of the languages.

Each time I made my way through a border crossing area, I noticed that our U.S. Border Patrol agents were engaged and busy most of the time. There were very few occasions when I would see an agent just standing around doing nothing. In addition, despite their heavy workload, the agents on the U.S. side of the crossing points were cordial and friendly. If I had a question, they answered me in a very polite manner and with a very positive attitude. The United States side of the border was also clean and neat in appearance; almost without exception, it was quite different when I left U.S. soil and drove into Mexico.

It had been several years since I'd been in Mexico—twenty-three years, to be exact—and I had a preconceived notion that conditions would be better than the last time I'd visited. But was I ever wrong. As far as I could see, there was no significant difference from the conditions that I had seen those many years before.

During one of my trips into Mexico, against my better judgment, I went into a border town at night. I did so because I wanted to complete the mission and get back home. Somehow, I got turned around and found myself driving down roads with no streetlights. I was lost in the barrio! To make matters worse, this town was known to have violent drug gangs.

As I drove, shop owners looked out their windows and smiled at me; people standing around on the streets just glared at me. Some stood around burn barrels, which was an interesting sight, considering the heat. I didn't notice what they were doing because I was busy trying to get back to the land of the free.

Something that stood out as I drove down one of those unlighted streets was that there appeared to be particulate matter floating around in the air. It was almost like looking at a very granular photograph. Apparently, the air was just very dirty. Anxiously, I continued to move through the streets until finally, I found my way back to the other side of the border.

Re-entering the U.S. was quite different from my passage into Mexico. On the Mexican side, all re-entry signs were written in Spanish. Moreover, the signs were typically filthy, as was much of what I encountered in Mexico; the filth would have made the signs hard to read even if I *could* understand Spanish.

As for the border guards on that side, the *Federales* had to be the most slovenly group of law enforcement officers I had ever seen. They were unkempt, with scraggly mustaches and dirty shoes. They typically hung out under shade trees, smoking cigarettes and doing absolutely nothing. Was I reassured that these guys were working very closely with the U.S. to control our common border through the president's proposed security and prosperity partnership (see Appendix I)? RIGHT! Sure I was.

The Mexican border guards who manned the tollbooths were typically non-responsive to verbal stimuli. I do not speak Spanish, but I tried to be respectful and say something to them in their native language, like "gracias" or "adios," along with my usual "have a great day" farewell. But they rarely even looked at me, much less checked my identification. Given this state of affairs, can you believe that our country is considering an agreement to place a common security perimeter around Mexico, the U.S. and Canada?

Going back into the United States was like driving out of the darkness and into the light, except for one very troubling thing: The U.S. border guards did not check for any identification, either. Typically, all that they would ask was, "Are you a U.S. citizen?" or "Where are you headed?"

It's my understanding that the U.S. government does not want to inconvenience travelers by making them wait at crossing points but outside of southern California, when I visited several of our ports of entry, I did not see any significant delays. It would appear that "inconvenience" is just another excuse that some in the government are using to cloud the issue. So what if people have to wait a little while in order to cross? We are engaged in a vicious war on terror, not to mention the other threats that are facing us from across our border, such as massive amounts of illicit drugs coming in every day and practically unchecked illegal immigration, which has resulted in approximately twelve million illegals in our country right now—or, at least, that is what we are repeatedly told. Whether Washington wants to admit it or not, Americans are up in arms over this issue.

And what makes these problems possible? What is it about our border with Mexico that makes drug and human trafficking so easy? To find out, I started with surveying the terrain conditions around the border crossing points. This was relevant to ascertaining the setting in which illegal immigrants, terrorists and drug traffickers could slip across undetected.

To do this, I parked on the side of the road and started walking, just taking in all the physical attributes of the land around me. Now, I served a great deal of time on contested international borders, and in all that time, I had never seen anything quite like our border with Mexico. The terrain along the border was quite varied—some areas were wide-open expanses and others were regions of close vegetation and heavy forestation; still others were improved areas such as cities and towns. Many areas offered natural concealment to anybody who wanted to illegally enter our country and not be detected; it would be next to impossible to find an intruder unless a Border Patrol agent happened to step on him.

I know what it's like to infiltrate a perimeter because I did it many times in the Army. Under the right conditions, you can crawl right up to somebody and he will not even know that you are there. Many of the areas I walked were perfect infiltration routes into the United States; with all the forestation, an illegal immigrant, a terrorist or a drug trafficker could walk for hundreds of miles without being seen. In the military, we called this type of terrain "perfect infantry country"—add rain to the mix and you'd have "perfect infantry weather," too.

After checking out the actual ground around the border to see what made it so easy to infiltrate, I talked with numerous Border Patrol agents to determine the facts from those who were on the ground, doing the heavy lifting. In my experience, the higher-ups have their perspective, and it is not always the same as the reality. If I wanted the truth, I knew that I had to get it from those in the trenches.

During my recon, I drew on my experience in the military. The border agents all knew what an inspector general was, so consequently, many cooperated with me. I do not present the following information in the actual form of the discussions that I had with these agents; instead, I mention some of my questions and the most frequent responses—the trends, if you will. These are just the highlights:

Do you believe that we have a problem controlling our border with Mexico?

"They're everywhere."

"They come in every kind of way."

"There are not enough of us to stop very many of them."

"We are overwhelmed."

"There's only so much we can do."

What has been the effect of the National Guard soldiers that the president ordered to the border?
"What National Guard soldiers?"
"Yeah, I heard about that, but I haven't seen any."
"There are some around, but they aren't doing much from what I can see."

I have read that there is a problem with border agent turnover. Is that a function of wages?
"No, the pay isn't that bad."
"I have been shot, shot at, knifed, jumped, mugged, spit on and bitten."
"Where's all this backup we've been hearing about?"
"We try and try and don't seem to be getting anywhere. That's very frustrating."

What is your opinion of putting our military on the border?
"Yeah, I guess that would work."
"Maybe if they were guarding the border, we could spend more time on what we normally do."

Like what?
"Inspections and stuff like that, ya know."

What is your opinion of a fence along the border?
"By itself, that won't mean much."
"We would have to have the manpower to make that work."
"Can we really put a fence along the whole border?"
"They'll just come in another way."

Which other way would they come in?
"Where there is a will, there is a way. Trust me."
"They come in through the airports."
"They will always find ways to get in."

The following short exchange dovetails with the frustration that many Border Patrol agents experience. This time, they were asking the questions, and I was giving the answers:

> "You said you were in the military, right?" one asked.
>
> "Yes, I was in the Army." I replied.
>
> "Okay, so when you were in foreign countries, how did they enforce their borders?"
>
> I explained, "You either have the proper paperwork or you don't get in. And if you are in a country and don't have the proper paperwork, such as an expired Visa, you go to jail."
>
> "There ya go. Why aren't we doing that?"

Based on my data set, which consists of observations made at several border-crossing points and interior checkpoints, during discussions with several Border Patrol agents and during my survey of the terrain, I arrived at the following initial conclusions:

1) The security of our border with Mexico is practically non-existent. Some major ports of entry have what appears to be adequate security in close proximity. However, a couple miles away, it is wide open.
2) Our border personnel are well-intentioned, and they are attempting to do the best they can with the resources that they have at hand. However, the areas in which they work are grossly undermanned.
3) The frustration that many agents expressed to me is understandable. They hear about reinforcements or that we are going to erect barriers along the border, but in many cases, they are not seeing these things getting done. Add this to the fact that many of them are constantly under assault, and they are not likely to engage in

armed confrontation without adequate support. In addition, they hear about security in other nations and fail to understand why we cannot strengthen our own borders.

4) The Mexican and U.S. governments are apparently not committed to securing our common border. The fact is that neither side pays much attention when someone crosses into America—much less do they verify identification.
5) I saw no evidence that supports the government's arguments about why we cannot or should not adequately defend ourselves from the threats that are coming at us from Mexico.

And given all of this, I determined that it would be worthwhile to investigate further. I started with an examination of the Mexican drug trade, and how its deadly goods are making their way into our country.

Chapter Two

Drug Trafficking

Plain and simple, the Mexican government allows drug traffickers to operate out of its country, and that is a direct threat to the United States.

These drug traffickers are not just gangs of junkies distributing their poison from the street corners anymore. Some drug organizations bring in more revenue than the economies of entire nations. In fact, drug trafficking generates $65 billion for Mexico each year, making it their number-one industry.[1]

What's more, these drug cartels are getting rich from *our* inaction. They employ military forces of their own to secure their operating areas and they're going more and more high-tech in their operations. One example of what many like to refer to as "paramilitary forces" is the Los Zetas, many of whom are ex-Mexican military, often special forces soldiers who received at least some of their training at the U.S. Army Infantry Center and School at Fort Benning, Georgia. However, their force composition is becoming more robust and lethal with the aggressive recruitment of Guatemalan special forces military personnel, known as *Kaibiles*, and the notorious *Maras*.[2]

But these are not purely paramilitary forces, as the mainstream media would have us believe. These are drug cartels with trained military soldiers supporting their operations. In the early '80s, one cartel even attempted to purchase two Russian military helicopters and a Tango-class patrol submarine to support their trafficking operations in and through the eastern Pacific Ocean.[3]

More recently, in December 2007, the United States Coast Guard discovered that drug traffickers are using submarines to transport illicit drugs through the Caribbean to the United States. These vessels can carry upwards of twelve tons of illicit drugs and are difficult for our surface forces to detect with current sensor arrays because they have a different signature than a more conventional submarine.[4]

Again, these are non-national entities employing their own militaries and obtaining advanced military hardware to support their operations against the United States. This means that we can no longer look only at other sovereign nations as being friend or foe. Just as we do with al-Qaeda, we need to look at the militarized, non-national entities working around the world to determine if we have threats that we must counter.

At present we have two major drug cartels operating throughout the Western hemisphere: the Gulf Cartel, run by Osiel Cardenas (currently in jail) and the Sinaloa Cartel, run by Joaquin Guzman. The Los Zetas work for Cardenas' Gulf Cartel, and there is yet another cartel run by Pablo Rayo-Montano, a reputed drug kingpin. But for the most part, the Gulf and Sinaloa cartels are the two real powers.

The military forces of these cartels are arguably not only paramilitary forces, but regular armed forces as well. And as time goes on, they continue to train people who enter into the combat forces that support the drug cartels. The Gulf and Sinaloa cartels are currently fighting for control of the town of Nuevo Laredo, just across Texas' border with Mexico. Why? Simple: It's a major staging area for the follow-on shipment and distribution of illicit drugs into the United States.

So, my question is, what can we do about this? Or, what *should* we do about this? I sincerely believe that we owe something to all of the otherwise innocent people who happen to be born into corrupt and shameless countries. These people live under leaders and a social "power elite" who are totally devoid of any compassion for their own countrymen. We have already acknowledged the reality that many of these nations are functionally in league with one another to take the U.S. for all it is worth. Consequently, we have to be firm and decisive with them, or nothing will ever change. Unless we take a strong stand—say what we mean and mean what we say—they will continue with business as usual.

I believe that we should lay the situation out for these countries and then solicit their genuine support in solving the problems that are facing us all. I know that we are currently engaged in counter-drug operations in many of the hot spots located south of our border, but apparently, our plan of action is not vigorous enough. I will give the president of the U.S. his due respect regarding the decisive operations we're conducting in the war on terror, but his leadership is weak on the dangers we face when it comes to the drug trade because we refuse to defend ourselves against the threats that are coming at us primarily through our own porous borders.

I believe that we have been more than fair and compassionate with our neighbors and that we have tried to lift them out of the squalor in which they live, but there comes a time when we have to say, "Enough is enough." No more carrots for those who fail to modify their own internal state of affairs.

An example: Knowing that Mexico is fundamentally corrupt, we have to start to replace the carrots with big sticks. One of those sticks should be in the form of combat operations to counter the drug cartels that are operating along our southern borders. How long do we have to keep getting kicked by these degenerates before we stand up and defend ourselves?

A case in point there is the Mara Salvatrucha-13. This violent gang is one of several threats taking root throughout our homeland. Translated into English, "Mara Salvatrucha" means "street-tough Salvadoran," and the number thirteen is the gang's street designation in Southern California. Most people abbreviate the name of the gang to "MS-13," "Mara," "MS" or "Posse."

As an aside, I want to mention that while I was in Costa Rica conducting additional reconnaissance on Costa Rica's economic progress compared to the rest of Latin America, I asked the locals the meaning of "Mara Salvatrucha." They put a different spin on the term, stating that it had to do with a trout, a very fast-moving and vigilant fish—this was their translation of "trucha." As fate would have it, I entered into this discussion with a Costa Rican who had been recently deported from Florida for drug trafficking, and he added that the term was commonly used in the Salvadoran military because the trout was always watching and moved very quickly.[5]

MS-13 had its beginnings in Los Angeles among Salvadoran emigrants. It currently boasts an estimated 50,000 members operating in Central America and another 10,000 in North America. They also have operations in Guatemala, Honduras, Belize, Mexico, Canada and at least thirty of our U.S. states, and are starting to have a presence in Europe.

These people are thugs in the purest sense, and they have training in firearms and explosives. Their main illegal activities include narcotics, extortion, arms dealing, prostitution and illegal immigrant smuggling. While researching this notorious organization, I discovered an appalling euphemism that is often used in the media when referring to their illegal activities: the word "business" or, better yet, their "business model." What are we trying to do, legitimize the heinous criminal conduct in which this gang is involved? Does everything have to be so politically correct? These are not nice people, and their criminal activities should not be referred to as doing "business."

I trust that our immigration officials are checking potential legal immigrants for the telltale MS-13 tattoos and denying entry to those with such markings. It does not matter if the ACLU and other leftist groups call it profiling; if someone wears the insignia on their skin, they are no longer candidates for legal immigration into the United States. The utter stupidity of political correctness is close to destroying our nation.

The problem is that we are not serious about defending the American public against this scourge because we will not properly defend our borders. Maybe we should consider sending some aid to the Sambra Negra, the "Black Shadow," because they hunt these MS-13 guys down in El Salvador.

I can hear the protests now: "Oh no, we can't do that! Black Shadow is a *vigilante* group!" But what are people supposed to do when they are overrun by criminals who have no concern for the rule of law, and their government is incapable of or unwilling to contain the threat?

At present, gangs such as these play a large part in the influx of drugs into our country. In response, the United States talks about the war on drugs, and much of what our government is attempting to do makes sense. We are currently conducting counter-drug operations in many countries and have law enforcement agencies in place to enforce our drug laws; we even have treatment facilities available for those who have drug problems.

When you look at the picture of the war on drugs, we have some significant efforts that are ongoing on many fronts—but we have one absolutely untenable position that is making many of these other efforts close to futile, one huge gap in the plan: Specifically, there is not enough security along our borders to keep the stuff from getting in here in the first place.

Now, I am a proponent of prevention rather than trying to pick up the pieces after the damage has already been done. What I mean by this is that we should be preventing the drugs from entering our country to begin with, rather than using our scarce law enforcement resources to track down the transgressors after the drugs are already here. I know that it may not be that easy, but we have to do something more, and we have to do it quickly. These drug cartels have absolutely no mercy, and they will stop at nothing to spread their poison in our country.

According to the Central Intelligence Agency's *The World Factbook*, Mexico is a "major drug producing nation."[6] It continues to produce and traffic heroin, marijuana, methamphetamine, ecstasy and cocaine. Can you guess which country is the biggest client of the drug syndicates that operate in and through Mexico? Of course, it is the United States.[7]

Leftists always like to argue that much of the situation in which we find ourselves is our own fault, but I beg to differ. I understand that all any American has to do is "just say no" to drugs, but apparently, that approach alone is not working. The leftist or progressive rationale seems to be that if we eliminate the demand for drugs, the drug producers will stop producing them and trafficking them into America. This makes some sense, but it has not been and will never be effective because the drug dealers do not play fair.

Another way to assuage the problem is to continue the interdiction operations—i.e., destroy the drug-related crops, assist foreign countries in replacing drug crops with other needed agriculture, dismantle the drug syndicates, and assist the noble efforts of those who are seriously trying to rid their countries of corrupt officials. I fully support all these efforts. I would like to see them increased even further.

However, we have been doing these things for years, and we are still not winning the war on drugs. For example, despite the fact that Mexico leads the largest illegal crop eradication effort in the world, it continues to cultivate opium poppy in an area of about 5,500 hectares, which translates to a potential of about twenty-three metric tons of "black tar" heroin. It also grows approximately 5,800 hectares of marijuana and is the number-one foreign supplier of marijuana and methamphetamine to the United States.

On top of that, the CIA states that Mexico is "the primary transshipment country for US-bound cocaine from South America, with an estimated 90% of annual cocaine movements towards the US." It also notes that "major drug syndicates control [the] majority of drug trafficking throughout the country" and that Mexico is a "significant money-laundering center."[8]

And the crimes don't stop there. Since 2006—the same year that President Felipe Calderon was elected—Mexico has seen over 4,152 deaths due to drug-related violence. This includes not just your average people on the street but soldiers, cops and attorneys as well. What's more, violence along the border is increasing, with 892 acts perpetrated against border agents from October 2007 to August 2008 alone. That's compared to 335 *total* in 2001.[9]

These numbers, needless to say it, are staggering—a word that's also often used in discussions of Iraq War casualties. Eerily, the latest Pentagon report shows the total number of US military fatalities to be 4,149,[10] a mere three people short of Mexico's statistic. The difference? In Iraq, it took five years to kill that many; in Mexico, it took only two.

The National Association of Former Border Patrol Officers keeps track of online press coverage of drug-related violence in Mexico, Central America and South America. In one of their recent reports, they noted not only the "basic" shootouts and executions but other disturbing scenarios including:

- Fifteen organized-crime-related murders in twenty-four hours, including a young victim who had been tied with wire and decapitated in the open—though the beheading was only partial because somebody came along and scared the killers off.
- Three men found in an abandoned, bullet-riddled SUV. They had been handcuffed to the seats and blindfolded, and there were signs of torture. In the end, they had been shot to death with an assault rifle.
- Discovery of a "narco grave" containing the remains of six bodies, two of whom might have been missing police officers.
- Two male murder victims whose faces had been taped. They had been beaten and repeatedly shot.

- A judge found in his home, lying face-down with his hands and feet tied. He had been beaten to death.
- At least twenty police officers in Mexico murdered by organized crime in the first seventeen days of 2008.
- Three hundred eighteen carjackings in Suarez in 2007.
- Execution of the chief of the La Mesa division of the Tijuana police by an armed group.

It seems as though every day, there's more and more lawlessness south of the border, and so much of it has to do with the production, sales and trafficking of illegal drugs. How can anyone in the United States today turn a blind eye on how this is affecting *our* country as well?

As I've said many times, I believe in the old saying, "An ounce of prevention is worth a pound of cure." It makes complete sense to me that if we were to prevent the entry of illegal drugs into our country in the first place, we would be able to decrease our efforts elsewhere—that is, we wouldn't have to put so much resources toward interdiction, making arrests and rehabilitating addicts, and there wouldn't be such a drag on our legal system from processing the drug dealers and users. In other words, if we could keep the bad guys and their evil product out in the first place, we could spend less money on fixing the problems.

According to the National Institutes of Health's National Institute on Drug Abuse, illegal drug addiction costs American taxpayers an estimated $161 billion a year.[11] While it's true that we continue to chip away at the network of transnational, illicit-drug organizations that supply an estimated 19.5 million illegal drug users in the United States—a number that includes a 500,000-user increase in the last year—there is more that we can do to combat this scourge on our society. I submit that if we want to get serious about the war on drugs, there are two areas on which we should focus.

The first action we must take is to modify our current federal anti-drug initiative, which has two primary elements: reducing demand and reducing supply.[12] My assessment of the current implementation of this initiative is that we are losing the war by trying to reduce the demand for drugs in the United States, and that we are having limited success regarding reduction of supply. Just one example of this is how, according to the State Department,

"Andean cultivation [of illicit-drug-related crops] has remained relatively stable in the past decade despite U.S. efforts"; in fact, "farmers are finding ways to increase productivity per unit of land."[13]

Another glaring deficiency in our current federal anti-drug initiative is that it offers no provision for decisive denial of transshipment of illicit drugs into our country. As a result, transnational, illicit-drug organizations are continuing to bring their products into the United States. This situation is getting even more serious as the drug traffickers are starting to align with terrorist groups and government organizations such as the Mexican military and police that perform escort duty for drug traffickers as they bring their drugs into the United States.[14] Therefore, my second recommendation for an area of focus: adding to the existing federal anti-drug initiative a means of denying cross-border transshipment of illicit drugs.

Until such measures are undertaken, however, we only have the current U.S.-international narcotics control strategy to work with. Largely, this involves the threat or application of sanctions against nations that produce and/or traffic drugs. The law on international drug control certification procedures requires that the president submit a report to Congress each year that identifies which countries are major drug traffickers or producers. In the report, the president must designate each country that has "failed demonstrably" to meet its counter-narcotics obligations; these designated countries can then become ineligible for foreign aid unless the president determines that the assistance is vital to U.S. national interest or that the country in question has made "substantial efforts" to improve its counter-narcotics performance.[15]

Now, I have already addressed the enormous role that Mexico plays in the international drug trade, so my question is, why isn't Mexico decertified under this procedure? Answer: The test is too subjective, and the president can easily circumvent the prerequisites for certification. When we assess Mexico against the decision parameters for certification, we have to take into consideration that while Mexican authorities have made some strides in crop eradication and have arrested key drug-trafficking personnel, ninety percent of U.S.-consumed cocaine still comes across the U.S.-Mexico border. In light of this, it's apparent that:

1. Mexico has "failed demonstrably"

2. Assistance to Mexico is not vital to U.S. national interest
3. Mexico has not made substantial efforts to improve its counter-narcotics performance

I recommend that the U.S. Congress take control of this certification process and decertify Mexico immediately. Until we hold Mexico (and the other countries that are doing us harm) accountable, we will never come close to winning the war on drugs. Yet, the government we have elected turns a blind eye to the evils that are causing havoc in our social order and knowingly puts our citizenry at the mercy of unscrupulous criminals and the country that harbors them. How often do we elect seemingly normal, good people to represent us only to have them "go native" once they get to the state capital or to Washington? I believe that the lobbyists, the special interests and the big government power elites mesmerize them.

I believe that there is a lack of real leadership on this subject and that we, as Americans, must stand up for what is right on this issue and begin to make change happen. The primary means of change is empowering voters, through education, to vote for people who are willing to do what their constituencies want and need them to do.

Chapter Three

Terrorism

Make no mistake: Terrorism is an extreme threat facing our nation. However, we need to remember that we are making headway, and not just abroad. Based on an intelligence briefing I received in the military, our internal security forces are stopping an average of one terrorist-related event per day in this country. That's a truly remarkable statistic considering all the ways in which terrorists can kill us. It's important to commend the amazing work being done by our combined agencies under the Department of Homeland Security, in conjunction with the efforts of our nation's military.

It is essential that we continue to fight terrorists abroad, as opposed to fighting them here at home. By fighting them in their own countries, we can continue to thwart their abilities to attack us in America on a timetable of their choosing. In addition, when we are on their "home turf," we can gather intelligence and keep an eye on what they are doing—a very close eye. Though counter-insurgency groups are often widely disbursed, making them difficult to find, that does not stop us from tracking their movements, recognizing when they are concentrating and, believe it or not, allowing that to happen. Letting them all get together in one place is often to our advantage—it makes it easier for us to come in and finish them off.

Even though there are more threats to our nation's security than terrorism, none of the other threats have the same potential for complete and immediate catastrophe. Think about it: On September 11, 2001, nineteen terrorists were able to hijack commercial airliners, use them as weapons and kill 3,000 people. It only takes one individual with a suitcase-sized nuclear device or a vial full of a deadly virus inside our country to carry out an attack of biblical proportion on innocent people.

Information from U.S. Citizenship and Immigration Services (USCIS) indicates that deportable aliens are coming into the U.S. from Afghanistan, Iraq, Kuwait, Lebanon, Pakistan, Saudi Arabia, Syria, Turkey, Yemen, Egypt, and Sudan—all known terrorist states.

Further, several chief law enforcement officers from border states, speaking before the Senate Judiciary Committee on March 1, 2006, warned that Arabic-speaking people were learning Spanish, integrating into the Mexican culture, and then hiring smugglers to bring them into the United States. In one news report, law enforcement officers warned that such individuals were likely terrorists and that drug cartels and even members of the Mexican military were helping them get across the border.[16]

Further, Sheriff Arvin West of Hudspeth County, Texas, said that there was no doubt in his mind that Mexican soldiers were working with the drug cartels to help terrorists gain entrance into the U.S., even though the Mexican and American governments adamantly deny it.[17]

This is just the tip of the iceberg. Both Canadian and U.S law enforcement officials are arresting more and more potential terrorists before they are able to carry out their heinous attacks. Law enforcement in Florida arrested a seven-member group—five of whom were U.S. citizens; one was a resident alien and one was an illegal immigrant—with its sights set on blowing up the Sears Tower in Chicago. In addition, a seventeen-member group was arrested by Canadian officials in Ontario.[18]

But again, we have to look outside our own borders. I wonder how many people know that when the Soviet Union collapsed, the Soviets lost positive control over several suitcase-sized nuclear devices. Or, moreover, that because the situation there was so desperate, many government and military officials sold off their military hardware on the black market. I consider all of this to be extremely dangerous for America and her allies. Who knows how much of these missing goods could make its way into North America?

The price of not having secured borders, I believe, is incalculable because of the enormous loss of life that could result from just one terrorist who enters our country. Despite this, it appears that the United States and her allies are leaning toward loss of the initiative, again, in the Middle Eastern theater of operations in the global war on terror. When we attacked our nation's enemies in Afghanistan and then in Iraq, some neighboring countries in the region were willing to either assist our efforts or, at least, stay out of the way—including Iran, by the way.

However, now that we have allowed our combat operations to degenerate to nothing more than law enforcement operations—which is not the long-term role or mission of our ground combat forces—the enemy is starting to set the conditions and tempo of battle. In other words, we are no longer taking the fight to a bewildered and overwhelmed enemy; we are actually allowing the enemy to take the fight to our forces. We are slipping back into reaction mode as we try to gain time for Iraq to stand on its own. No doubt, the surge operations were having a positive effect, but if we dial down these operations too soon, we'll be right back where we were.

During the 2006 and 2008 election cycles, we heard repeated calls from the Democrats to pull out of Iraq. Now that the Democrats have a majority in both houses of Congress and there is a Democrat in the White House, this may be the course of action our country pursues in the very near future. However, I believe that if we withdraw our military forces before we thoroughly defeat our enemies, we will lose the war. Such a move by our nation is nothing short of surrender. Worse yet, we will be placing Iraqis, as well as other people of the free world, at grave risk.

To put this into context, remember that when we surrendered in Vietnam, the Communists killed millions of people in the region—people who had trusted America to save them from the Communist scourge. Are we willing to abandon yet another people and allow them to be slaughtered by the Islamic aggressors?

Perhaps we are, because all we keep hearing from the "experts" is that we cannot stay the course, and that a surge is not the answer. But what solutions have these experts been offering? Ah, yes: surrender. Our elected politicians seem to be, more often than not, very short on real solutions and very long on meaningless rhetoric. I'm not surprised, because only a few members of Congress have served in the military.

Before getting into the particulars we must consider if we want to win the war in the Middle East, I want to share some thoughts on our current situation and tell you what "war" means.

We went to war in Afghanistan because al-Qaeda was operating out of that country, and they were the ones who attacked us. The reasons for expanding the global war on terror into Iraq are not at issue—but the fact that we are in Iraq is. We have to finish what we started there.

Now, we are at war. This makes me think back to our Civil War and the strategy used by generals Ulysses S. Grant, Philip Sheridan and William Sherman: waging total war. Basically, they determined that the only way to finally end the war was to take the fight to the enemy with ruthless determination—or else the war would continue to drag on.

The highlights of their strategy were denying the enemy's subsistence and livelihoods (destroying industry, crops and homes), no more paroles for prisoners of war and unrelenting pressure on the enemy—pursue, pursue, pursue. The Union Army was like a steamroller that crushed all resistance and burned everything in its wake.

What I described there is a horrible prospect, but it is war. General Sherman said that "war is hell," and he was right. If you are not willing to wage total war, then don't ever pull the trigger. Well, we pulled the trigger on Iraq, so now we must win.

As far as I'm concerned, to facilitate victory in the Iraqi campaign, we should begin by asking ourselves two questions:

1. Who are our friends in the Islamic world?
2. Who are our enemies in the Islamic world?

The answer to the first question is extremely short: Israel. The answer to the second question is, to be honest, everybody else. Why is Israel our only friend? This is also very simple to answer: It's the only country that is not Islamic. Lebanon is not entirely Islamic, but Hezbollah dominates it, so I will lump them in with the rest of the bad guys.

Our relationship with Israel is not an alliance of convenience. Israel is a nation that has fundamental social, religious and ideological similarities to the civilized, Western world. We must stand by them because they are deserving of our support, and because doing so is in our national interest.

From a purely strategic perspective, Israel is much like a forward bunker of freedom in the Middle East. Make no mistake about the fact that this nation is at the razor-sharp edge of the spear in the war against uncivilized nations that want to destroy the civilized world. For how long have Islamic nations been trying to destroy Israel? How about almost from the beginning of Israel's existence? Examples of this include the 1967 and 1973 Arab-Israeli wars, and Islamics continue to attack Israel at almost every turn. Just look at the recent rocket attacks launched against Israel from the Gaza Strip.

Islamic attackers have always met stiff resistance from the Israelis, and have been decisively defeated. Still, Islamics continue to harass and kill Israelis at every opportunity and it doesn't seem as though they're going to change. Leftists often like to say, "We can change minds through education and by ensuring that all people have an acceptable standard of living." That may be true in some cases, but this is not one of them.

Case in point: I recall talking to a group of well-educated Jordanian army officers who were of the opinion that the Israelis were after total conquest of the Middle East. When I asked them whether peace in the Middle East could ever be a reality, they said that they'd been trained all their lives to kill Jews, and that was what they were going to do. So, it appears that education isn't really the only answer.

It's also apparent that the Islamics do not desire peace with Israel—they only want its complete and total destruction. And yet, some say that Israel should consider trading land for peace? That does nothing but leave them, as a nation, more vulnerable.

Instead of trading land, the first step Israel should take is to seize all terrain that is necessary for its defense and ultimate survival. Israel has been trying to live in peace with its neighbors, but that will never work, and it's not worth the loss of even one more Israeli life to try to do so. Israel must consolidate its position so as to reduce vulnerability—i.e., take back the West Bank and the Gaza Strip, never even consider giving the Golan Heights back to Syria, and expand into the Sinai as far as necessary to facilitate defense. Furthermore, it must expand buffer zones around the entire perimeter of the country, construct obstacles to secure that perimeter and absolutely control who enters the nation.

Another component of Israel's strategy should be potential expulsion of all Islamic people who are not willing to peaceably coexist with the Israelis. This may seem a bit harsh, but remember that the Israelis have been bending over backward for these people, not to mention being slaughtered by them, for many decades and there comes a time when enough is enough.

For our part in the matter, we have to realize that the same Islamic terrorists and regimes that have sworn to eradicate Israel have also vowed to destroy the United States and England. After all, in the mind of the Islamic world, the United States is the "Big Satan" and Israel is the "Little Satan." Is there really any way to reason with these people? The answer is "no," because they are bigots.

It doesn't matter how much the mainstream media and the leftist elites want to sugarcoat the situation; the Islamics are not our friends, period. Islamic countries with which we have seemingly favorable relations are primarily friendly to us at their convenience—countries like Saudi Arabia and Kuwait, who want to sell us their oil and have our protection.

A broad approach that could lead to victory in the Iraq theater of operations (ITO) should include holding the aggressor nations accountable for their actions and providing a clearly defined mission to the combatant commander in Iraq. In order to hold the aggressor nations accountable, we must identify who they are. The most obvious are Iran, Syria and Lebanon, which is again a country dominated by Hezbollah.

When I hear people say that we've gotten ourselves involved in another Vietnam, I find myself agreeing with them for two primary reasons. First, we're allowing other nations to aid, abet and harbor our enemies. Second, the leftists and mainstream media are successfully chipping away at public opinion in a concerted attempt to undermine the war effort. These same things happened during the Vietnam War.

Going back to those two questions we need to answer if we want victory in Iraq, once we've identified the nations that are against us, we should initiate diplomatic communications with each of them. You may think that you know where this is going, but hang on a minute. The only reason we should take the time to have diplomatic relations with these countries is to inform them that we are going to treat them either as our friends or as our enemies—that they are either part of the solution or part of the problem. And if one of those nations decides to be a part of the problem, then we must take overwhelming combat action to modify its behavior. You may recall that President Reagan used such an approach with Libya—and that it worked. As a matter of fact, it's still working.

When people want to kill us, the lives of our combat forces are at stake, as well as the lives of countless innocent people. The only answer is to kill the direct enemies of our nation first—no lawyers, no world court, no trials and I don't want to hear about "proportionality" either. We can gain peace through strength.

Along with these negotiations, we must isolate the battle area—basically, in this instance, the country of Iraq. This has to be a precursor to any action we take if we want to achieve decisive results.

The next order of business is for the National Command Authorities to provide a clearly defined mission to the overall combatant commander on the ground in Iraq. An appropriate task and purpose—critical elements of a mission statement—to include in that mission should be to destroy the enemy and its supporting systems (task), so as to advance peace and stability in Iraq (purpose). In addition, the ground commander must understand that we are no longer expecting our combat forces to be little more than policemen. This is war, and we want our forces to do what they do best: kill the enemy with unrelenting and overwhelming combat power.

Once the commander has a well-defined mission, he can further identify the combat operations that will be required of his subordinate commands. One possible tactic to consider is "cordon and clear," in which an area of operations is isolated to facilitate follow-on combat operations. In this circumstance, this means clearing Iraq of all enemy forces.

It may be essential to couple our cordon and clear operations with temporary relocation of the innocent civilians who live in the areas, so we can minimize the loss of innocent lives. Once an area is clear, we can begin the process of bringing the displaced people back to their homes. However, we must be extremely vigilant when we carry out the repopulation operations. What I mean by this is that we will have to strictly screen all personnel who are returning home.

Accounting for all displaced persons would entail screening them during the combat phase, removing suspected belligerents, and then only allowing those who we can absolutely be certain are not belligerents to return home. The last and ongoing phase of any such operation would necessarily be the maintenance of a secure perimeter to deny any enemy infiltration.

Chapter Four

Infectious Diseases

Tracking down specifics on the potential effects that the flood of illegal immigrants is having on the health of Americans was exhausting. The problem doesn't seem to gain much press, I guess because there aren't many blatant outbreaks of disease in our country. However, there is substantial reason for alarm.

There is a plethora of information available regarding all sorts of diseases and illnesses in the national and international tracking systems managed by the Centers for Disease Control and Prevention (CDC), the Department of Health and Human Services (DHHS) and the World Health Organization (WHO). However, these organizations do not differentiate between illegal and legal immigrants when they collect data; the two categories are combined into one called the "foreign born."

During the research phase of this project, I came across an analysis that was put together by Madeleine Cosman, Ph.D. Through her study, published in the *Journal of American Physicians and Surgeons,* I discovered that there are grave health issues lurking in our country. I intentionally use the word "lurking" because the potential health threats include bacteria, fungi, parasites and viruses—dangers that are not always obvious. When illegal immigrants enter our borders carrying them, they may appear healthy, but the bad news is that many of them are far from it.

During my time in the military, I traveled to and lived in many foreign countries, and, in my experience, with very few exceptions, other nations' health standards just are not acceptable. They are so far below America's standards that they are virtually nonexistent. Many countries still contend with tuberculosis, polio, leprosy, intestinal parasites, malaria—and the list could go on. With the massive influx of immigrants to the U.S., the same problems are beginning to crop up within our own nation once again.

Some points of particular import:

- Multi-drug-resistant tuberculosis (MDR TB) is resistant to at least the two main first-line TB drugs. It is also approximately sixty percent fatal. Ordinary TB is usually cured in six months for about $2,000, but MDR TB takes up to twenty-four months, at a cost of about $250,000. Each infected immigrant in the U.S. has the potential to pass the disease on to ten to thirty unsuspecting Americans.[19]
- Hansen's disease, better known as leprosy, is on the rise in America. In a forty-year period, ending in 2002, we had 900 total cases of leprosy in the United States. However, from 2002 through 2004, 7,000 cases were reported.[20]
- Polio had been eradicated in America, but it's now making a comeback through illegal immigrants.[21]
- Malaria was obliterated, but now it is re-emerging in Texas.[22]
- Hepatitis A, B, and C are resurging.[23]

I want to mention again that during my research into this area of concern, the data was not readily obtainable, and what was out there was rather sparse. I became frustrated while searching for information in the CDC, DHHS and WHO archives. Honestly, I had no success correlating the location of the preponderance of illegal immigrants and the rates of infectious diseases in those areas. However, it makes sense to me that with the frequency of disease in many of the countries that are primary sources of illegal immigrants that come to our country, there should be some reason for concern.

When people come here legally, they have to go through a health screening process. This is very important because we have to ensure that we do not subject our population to serious harm. Having lived in various foreign countries over the years, I can tell you that America is so clean that when Americans travel in some of these foreign countries, we must take special care; there are bacteria and other nasty things out there that do not seem to harm the locals but can be extremely detrimental to our health. We simply do not have the same immune system antibodies that they do to combat all vectors of infectious diseases. Thinking back to when I was stationed in the Republic of Korea (ROK)—better known to many as South Korea—I recall seeing many people wearing surgical masks. When I asked why, I was told that it was because they did not want to catch TB. Moreover, service personnel were strictly screened for TB before departing for duty in the ROK and before returning to the United States.

Some of the diseases that are much more prevalent in Central and South America are tuberculosis, hepatitis A and B, syphilis, gonorrhea and one that I had never heard of until I came across it in my research: a rather sinister affliction called Morgellons disease. Is it only coincidence that in the U.S., Morgellons is primarily reported in California, Florida, and Texas? Consider that these states are home to, by and large, the lion's share of the illegal immigrants in this country, and the words of Steve Radack, commissioner of the Harris County hospital district in Houston, Texas. He said, "Untreated infectious diseases among immigrants might spread to the broader population if they aren't treated."[24] If that's true for Texas, then wouldn't it be true for any other state with an illegal immigrant population as well? Connect the dots and see what you conclude.

Some of the diseases coming across our borders are not considered communicable. However, some diseases, like tuberculosis, are very real threats to the health of our citizens. Moreover, even though what they're bringing along may not be readily communicable, there are other negative effects when disease carriers enter this country. A main concern is the drain that continuing to allow people to come in without health screenings could put on the American health care system. Illegal immigrants overburdening the system could lead to American citizens who are in need of health services not receiving what they need in a timely manner.

So, one would assume that proper health screenings would be the answer, yet this is not necessarily the case. Studies have found that even legal migrants to the United States have caused TB caseloads to increase because they were infected before leaving their countries of origin. One study found that thirty-one to forty-seven percent of migrant farm workers tested on the east and west coasts of the United States were TB positive, and that those groups were six times more likely to develop TB than the general population.[25] This begs the question: Why are we allowing them to enter?

According to the *Journal of the American Medical Association* (JAMA), instances of TB are on the rise in America.[26] Can you guess which states have the highest incidence of the disease? Try California, New York, Texas, Florida, New Jersey and Illinois, and except for New Jersey, these states have the highest concentrations of illegal immigrants in our country. Do you think there may be some reason why there are so many cases of TB in these particular locations?

According to the JAMA article, "Approximately two thirds of these cases were originally from Mexico, the Philippines, Vietnam, India, China, Haiti, and South Korea."[27] Considering that current estimates put Mexico at the top of our illegal immigration list, sending us eighty-nine percent of all illegal immigrants in our country, we have to do something to stem the flood of unchecked people entering the United States.

Interestingly, though, the JAMA article, makes no mention of legality or illegality when it discusses the presence of immigrants in the U.S.; the subjects are simply referred to as "foreign-born persons" or "immigrants." However, as already pointed out, whenever legal immigrants come to our country, they are examined for infectious diseases before they are admitted. Therefore, it would be quite logical to conclude that most of these documented TB cases are coming into our nation via illegal immigrants, rather than through regular, legal immigrants. However, we would not want anybody to think that the illegal immigrants in this country are the problem, now would we? It would seem that political correctness prevails in that JAMA report.

Another study, done by the CDC, states that "tuberculosis is a leading public health problem and a recognized priority for the federal governments of both Mexico and the United States of America."[28] In their analysis, incidences of TB in the four border states with Mexico (Texas, New Mexico, Arizona and California) were examined and compared with the incidence rates for the other forty-six states within the union. They discovered that 76.7 percent of the TB occurrences were localized in the four border states.[29]

Part of that same study reveals that more often than not, Mexican-born patients with TB had an increased propensity for resistance to treatment. The CDC concluded that this was because Mexican-born patients did not always comply with the medication regimen that was necessary to prevent TB carriers from infecting others.[30] In other words, we try to treat these people for a disease that will kill them if left untreated—a disease that is highly communicable in certain environments—and they don't even take the medicine that we give them. How irresponsible can a person be? It is very selfish of them not to take whatever steps are necessary to safeguard the health of those around them.

Among the WHO's emerging concerns are virulent strains of TB that are even more resistant than MDR TB, which I mentioned earlier. Known as XDR TB, or extensive drug-resistant tuberculosis, these strains were first classified by the WHO in 2006. They are essentially the same as MDR TB but with added resistance to three or more of the six classes of second-line drugs.[31]

This is of particular concern because when such a hideous disease develops resistance to the very drugs that are supposed to combat it, the implications for all of us are enormous. As I mentioned earlier, when people follow the prescribed medication regimen, they can recover successfully; it's when we have to continually treat and retreat that the TB gains resistance. Essentially, if patients discontinue their antibiotic treatment before all of the TB is killed, the surviving infection can mutate and become more resistant to that same form of treatment.

Personally, I do not care why people might fail in their duty toward their fellow man by discontinuing the appropriate medical treatment for TB. The fact is, these people are endangering the lives of others, and we need to do everything we can, as a sovereign nation, to protect our population by preventing such people from crossing our borders. The CDC study I referenced earlier also found cases of TB that are so resistant to our first- and second-line drugs, the TB is virtually untreatable. This serious, recent data demonstrates that the incidence of resistant TB is on the rise in the United States.

I know no other way to put this: We had better pay attention to this situation now and quit playing "patty cake" with those who remain ignorant of the damage they are causing other people—and those who care nothing for others, only for themselves.

Another emerging problem related to illegal immigration in the U.S. is the spread of HIV and AIDS—and not just in our country. HIV/AIDS is on the rise in many Mexican communities because their nationals contract the disease while in America and then take it back to Mexico when they visit their families. In some cases, it is apparent that migrant workers are getting infected in California and then exposing their wives to the disease when they are back in Mexico.

This is another reason why we must gain control over who enters and inhabits our country: to protect the population of Mexico. We must have regulated and comprehensive health screenings for all people who desire to immigrate to our country so that even foreign nationals are safe. No matter how this issue involves you and your family, health accountability and responsibility make good sense for everyone involved.

Chapter Five

Illegal Immigration

It is difficult to assess the magnitude of the illegal immigration problem in this country. According to statistics from the Department of Homeland Security, 960,756 illegal immigrants were apprehended by Border Patrol and Immigration and Customs Enforcement (ICE) in 2007—854,261 of which were from Mexico. That means that eighty-nine percent of the illegal immigrants fleeing to America are Mexicans.[32]

(As a side note, in case you are not aware, there is no longer an Immigration and Naturalization Service [INS] within the U.S. government. The agency has been rolled into U.S. Citizenship and Immigration Services [USCIS]; the ICE bureaus operate within the Department of Homeland Security.)

Another daunting task is trying to establish how many illegal immigrants, from *all* foreign nations, actually live and work in America today. The government throws figures around in the media as if they actually know how many are here, but the numbers they have are only estimates based on census data—their only real method, at this point in time, of assessing the illegal immigrant situation.

Let's look at how such data might be collected.

Two census workers knock on the door of a house where a number of illegal immigrants live. It's common for multiple illegal immigrants to live in the same dwelling for financial or cultural reasons, or to "hide out" from ICE agents who might try to enforce our country's laws—which would include discovering and deporting such people.

The illegal immigrants inside the house have heard the census takers' knock at the door. What do you suppose they'll do? I imagine they might remain quiet for some time, hoping that the strangers will just go away. But the census workers do not leave. Peeking out a window, one of the illegal immigrants sees them standing there on the steps, holding clipboards and looking quite official.

One of the census takers announces, "We are from the United States Census Bureau and we just want to ask you a few questions. Is there anybody home?"

Statistics indicate that many illegal immigrants in the U.S. are illiterate and uneducated due to the failed systems within their countries of origin, which probably left them with few opportunities at home. Furthermore, they probably harbored a healthy distrust of the corrupt governments back in their home countries. Given all this, now that they are in America, should they be expected to put their faith in U.S. governmental authorities?

Many would say "no," and that is the case when this houseful of immigrants sees the census takers outside their door. Like many other illegal immigrants, they do not open the door for these apparent government officials, thus already skewing the information that the census will have to work with. Inside, there were five, six, maybe twelve illegal immigrants that would not be counted in the census—which is, remember, the U.S. government's method of counting them.

Some illegal immigrants are not so fearful of official-looking U.S. citizens and do open their doors to the census takers. However, again, you can't expect their trust to be complete, or their responses to the census takers' questions to be completely honest. By definition, whatever life situations brought them to this country, they are here illegally; they are criminals. So how can we rely on them to answer our government's questions honestly?

Beyond that, the larger problem is that census takers are not allowed to verify a person's citizenship status during an interview—it's just too *politically incorrect*. They're only allowed to ask if the occupants are foreign-born, how long they have been here, and if they are U.S. citizens. They cannot ask for evidence that would betray the person's actual legal status. Again, how are we supposed to get an accurate count of illegal immigrants in this country if this is the only method of counting we've got?

Historical trends in illegal immigration demonstrate that the current flood we are experiencing began in 1996. Evidence suggests that there were twelve million illegal immigrants in the U.S. in 1981—information that was included in the Supreme Court's *Plyler v. Doe* opinion 1982[33]—but information on anything before that is scarce. The reason? When President Ronald Reagan granted amnesty to millions of illegals in 1986, they were effectively removed from the statistics as they were, simply, no longer illegal. We cannot count them in the estimated number of illegals in our country today.

A recent congressional report estimates that as many as ten million illegal aliens entered the U.S. in 2005 alone,[34] and we can assume that the numbers for 2006 were as high as or even greater than that—history does, after all, tend to repeat itself when there are discussions of another amnesty. Consider that there is a ten-percent detention rate of those who enter America illegally. We detained 1.1 million and 960,756 illegal immigrants in 2006 and 2007, respectively. That means that we could have had as many as twenty million illegal immigrants enter the U.S. during that one two-year period.

But, that's just an estimate, and it's just one of many. Everyone seems to have a guess as to how many illegal immigrants are in the U.S. at any given time, including:

- US Census Bureau: 8.7 million based on data from 2000.[35]
- USCIS: seven million as of 2003.[36]
- Bear Stearns Asset Management in New York: eighteen to twenty million as of 2006.[37]
- US Border Patrol union in Tucson, Arizona: fifteen million as of 2006.[38]
- Congressman Tom Tancredo (R-CO): twenty-five million as of 2006.[39]

And now, I'll throw mine into the mix. Considering the government's methodology in deriving its numbers and the validity of other available estimates,

I conclude that it is prudent to use an estimate that is somewhere around thirty-five million illegal immigrants in the United States.

Now, since I brought up the idea of amnesty, imagine the US government authorizing an amnesty program that would instantly legalize every one of these millions of unauthorized residents. The ripple effect of this would be phenomenal not just because it would increase our population drastically and suddenly, but because it would allow chain migration—a characteristic of our immigration and naturalization policy that was originally intended to keep families together but today serves to simply add to our country's overpopulation.

With chain migration, when an American marries someone from a foreign country, that foreign person can potentially bring into the United States his or her parents and adult siblings. In turn, they all can potentially bring in *their* children, *their* parents, and the adult children of *their* parents—we're talking nieces, nephews, aunts, uncles, the whole clan.

Let's take a closer look at the implications of this policy. Say a man marries a woman who has two parents and a brother. When the federal government allows the wife's immigration, it also allows three other people to immigrate if they so desire, so the wife is able to bring her three relatives into the country. Add in the fact that those parents have parents and siblings who are also eligible, as are any children they may have. If both sets of the wife's grandparents are living, that adds four more who can immigrate; if they each have two children besides the wife's parents, then that's four *more* who can get into the country legally.

This is a slippery slope that has the potential to grow out of control. Once the first immigrant comes into our country, they can potentially sponsor countless other immigrants as well. I can understand the compassionate nature of the original concept—to keep families together—but what this immigration policy has evolved into is simply not justifiable. These days, it's just another situation benefitting impoverished countries at the extreme expense of American taxpayers. Are we supposed to be the welfare state that supports the rest of the world?

Some would say "yes"—especially, perhaps, those who seek to be supported. Remember the marches staged by illegal immigrants in 2006? They were protesting proposed legislation HR 4437, which aimed to, among other things, make illegal immigration a felony both for the immigrants and for anyone who helped them enter the US. They were also demonstrating in support of a path to legalization for unauthorized immigrants already in this country.

In my opinion, these rallies were seditious in nature. Sedition is "activity aimed at inciting treason or some other lesser commotion against public authority."[40] Do you think that the people who participated in these rallies were concerned with the laws of our nation? Do you believe they wanted to try to change the minds of the American people through peaceable assembly? No, this was mob action. The leftists—the exploitative organizers of these marches—keep trying to sugarcoat the truth, but the fact still remains that many in this country care nothing for the rule of law. Regardless of what they profess, their actions speak much louder than their words.

As I watched and read about these protests in 2006, the words of our Founding Fathers came to mind. Again turning to *The Federalist Papers* for support, I found it readily apparent that their major reason for wanting a central government was to ensure the defense of this great nation against its foreign and domestic enemies—the factious elements in the society that could undermine our very existence. How better to describe those who seek to be rewarded for flagrantly breaking our country's laws?

Perhaps the most disturbing thing I saw in the press coverage of those rallies in 2006 was the people marching through our streets, carrying Mexican flags and shouting, "*Reconquista!*" (a move that the organizers of these rallies obviously saw as a tactical error; they quickly convinced the demonstrators to carry at least a few American flags for the sake of public relations).

This wasn't the first time I'd heard that word. It had come up during a conversation I'd had in 1992 with a military intelligence officer at the Command and General Staff College at Fort Leavenworth, Kansas. He'd been working in South America to monitor movements that might threaten the United States, and said that illegal immigration into the United States was deliberate. Mexico, as well as some other Central and South American countries, he said, even had a name for what they envisioned: They called it "*Reconquista*," a premeditated plan to *reconquer* the southwestern United States.

As I witness what is happening in our nation today, I am reminded of this word. *Reconquista* doesn't seem like people just wanting to live freely, does it? No, just the opposite, it sounds violent, combative and malicious—and, as I said before, seditious.

I can tell you that *reconquista* is going on right now within our borders. It is well-planned, perpetuated by some foreign governments and facilitated by our effectively open border with Mexico—another reason why our government really needs to get on the ball and remedy this situation.

Still, it does not. The people in our government seem to be dragging their heels, unsure of how to proceed against this increasingly overwhelming problem. Only the terrorist attacks of September 11, 2001 really made our politicians even begin to approach the border security problem. Before that full-scale attack on our own people, anyone trying to stand up for America and openly discuss these border issues was shouted down as a racist, a xenophobe or a bigot. Nothing was further from the truth, but these were typical labels that the progressives and the internationalists always threw at those who were trying to provide leadership in the area of international policy. Still today, these problems are tearing away at the very fabric and viability of our national existence. These exigent times require clear and decisive action—now rather than later.

After having traveled to many parts of the world I have concluded that average citizens do not hate us. The reality is that there are *governments* around the world who hate America, probably out of envy. We have to wake up to the fact that many foreign governments have hostile agendas concerning our nation. In short, we need to call these people out without fear of being called, as I mentioned earlier, xenophobes or bigots. We need to ignore the name-calling elements of our society who attempt to dominate the public debate through intimidation and make the hard decisions necessary to defend our nation from seditious people inside our borders and malicious elements throughout the world.

Within the United States, we must look at the foreign nationals whose motivations for being here are questionable. It adds insult to injury that many of these people are not even citizens of our country, and yet they're organizing as mobs and demanding that we legalize them as citizens. In their words, they want to reconquer our land by starting a so-called revolution. I understand that they want American citizenship as soon as possible, but that is not the way to go about it.

Perhaps that is part of the problem, though: that they want what they want right at this minute. This mentality seems to be an offshoot of today's convenience-driven society, where nothing worthwhile can ever take very long to complete or require too much effort, lest the people involved get too frustrated. When they do, they begin yelling, screaming and demonstrating—with the full backing of the mainstream media and the politicians who cave in to their demands.

But ironically, this *reconquista* idea shows that these people are not here to become Americans. They are here to benefit from what America can offer them while still retaining their own languages and cultures. This is quite different from immigrants who came to this country in previous centuries—proud immigrants primarily from the United Kingdom and her possessions. Today's group of invaders is here merely to plunder the riches of the "evil" United States for their own private gain, arguably with the assistance of their foreign governments. I tell you, sometimes I just get sick of hearing about how we are a "nation of immigrants."

As long as our politicians fail to lead, we cannot come out of this situation faring very well. During the 109th and 110th Congresses, there was and continues to be debate on amnesty proposals that are not reassuring. Considering that we may have as many as thirty-five million illegal immigrants in this country, amnesty could mean that we could have another sixty to 100 million legal immigrants in this country in a matter of a few years—which, of course, does not include any new, *illegal* immigrants who will come into our country in that same time period.

The sixty to 100 million figure would primarily result from the legalization of the current illegal population, increases to legal immigration quotas, and chain migration. This should be of significant concern to Americans because assimilating that number of people into our society while maintaining and preserving the values and traditions that define us as "America" will be next to impossible—and we, the taxpayers, will foot the bill for it.

Even so, our Congress could enact this legislation without letting the American people vote on it. I imagine that their decisions are instead made in some dark, smoke-filled back room where they mumble to each other in ridiculous, brain-numbing intonations, and then everybody comes out thinking that they have to consider "the bigger picture" and "the betterment of the entire world."

Our political system is becoming an absolute disgrace. I proudly appreciate that there are still some strong leaders out there, but they are woefully too few in number to hold back those politicians who continue to misrepresent our interests in state legislatures as well as in Congress.

What really needs to be examined, I believe, is not amnesty or so-called reform, but a moratorium on immigration. I believe that before we allow any more legal immigrants into the country—or before we start thinking about legalizing the illegals who are already here—it would be prudent to stop and assess our number of illegal immigrants and then develop an appropriate plan to rectify the situation we are in.

As part of that plan, I further propose that we consider not allowing Islamics to immigrate to America. If you consider the major social and military conflicts throughout the world, including, Afghanistan, Bosnia, Chechnya, Cyprus, East Timor, Ethiopia, Eritrea, India, Pakistan, Israel, Kosovo, Lebanon, Macedonia, Nigeria, the Philippines, Somalia, Sudan, Thailand and Uganda, the Islamics are the common thread throughout them all. Why should we let people who incite such violence into our country?

Well, you know, some say that only ten percent of Islamics are killers. So? That means that when we allow 10,000 of them to enter the US, only 1,000 of them will be potential terrorists. Does that sound acceptable to you?

I'll concede not *all* Islamics are out to kill us, but you have to admit that large numbers of them quite probably are. Is it worth risking American lives to have these people moving about freely in our midst just for the sake of multiculturalism? Where is it written that America must take all the risks associated with certain religious groups? Are we expected to buoy up the entire planet?

Do you remember the Islamic riots in France in early 2006? Destruction across the country; they burned an estimated 10,000 cars and firebombed 300 buildings.[41] How about when Australian Islamics demanded to live under Sharia law instead of the laws of the nation?[42] Similarly, in England, polling data indicates that as many as sixty-one percent of Islamics living there would prefer that civil cases within their own communities be adjudicated under Sharia principles.[43]

Are these the sort of things we want happening here? These examples are all representative of the Islamic separatist mindset, which is extremely dangerous. What happens when, after being allowed to enter the United States legally, their population reaches the point of majority and then carries out its desires through our own democratic processes?

Since I mentioned Australia, let's consider it for a moment. Australia typically has monetary requirements attached to its immigration policy. A person who wants to emigrate there, depending on his age, could have to pay in the neighborhood of $250,000 as a precursor to entry. In other words, he would have to buy his way into their system of social services. Consequently, Australia does not have the same systemic burdens as the United States.

And yet, despite this, the U.S. is expected to welcome people of all ages—especially thanks to chain migration, which facilitates the entry of countless older and elderly people. The American taxpayers are then expected to pick up the tab on the medical and Social Security costs that will go toward these people when they are U.S. citizens, further dragging the nation as a whole into economic hardship.

In my view, we could better help such people in their own countries, through humanitarian aid and by influencing political and economic change. For example, we could stem the flow of illegal immigrants from Mexico if we changed the way we deal with its corrupt government, which practically drives out its own people—and laughs at us as they flee to our country illegally. Even Mexican President Felipe Calderon acknowledged that he has relatives living here illegally.[44]

But how can we do this? How can we help other nations—most especially, the people of those nations—if we can't maintain the strength of our own economy and our Judeo-Christian, American culture? We've tried the leftist and globalist methods for decades. When are we going to learn that those flawed policies do not work? They only generate more of the same mess that we've already witnessed. Simply put, the best policy for us and for the world is for the United States to be as strong as possible, and to allow other countries to grow and strengthen on their own. We *all* will be much stronger as a result.

I offer further discussion of solutions to the illegal immigration problem later on, in Part III.

Chapter Six

Human Trafficking

Human trafficking is not a subject that people like to think about. We don't see it on the news every night; we don't hear about our government's great initiatives to combat it. There is no "war on human trafficking" and the presidential candidates did not have it on their slate of issues. But they should have. Because even though we do not like to think about it, just like the drug trade and illegal immigration, it's going on right under our noses—in an international market worth $32 billion every year.[45]

We can define human trafficking as the recruitment, transportation, delivery or receipt of people into a situation of involuntary servitude—including anything from forced, manual labor under slave-like conditions to prostitution or other sexual exploitation.[46] Victims of this heinous crime are often poor, unemployed and lacking a social support system, and, in some countries, are mostly women and children.[47]

Victims of human trafficking are sometimes abducted against their will and sometimes coerced through deception, threats of or actual violence, or the promise of a good job and a better life.[48] Often, debt restitution plays into it as well—the debt being the cost of their immigration or the price for which they have been bought, unbeknownst to them. What these people often find is that to "work it off" they will have to toil long hours under inhuman conditions, for little to no pay, with no end in sight.

Because of the underground nature of this crime, it's difficult to pin down the exact number of people it affects on an annual basis. The U.S. State Department, which prepares a yearly report on the topic, estimated in 2008 that two to four million people are trafficked within countries and across borders every year.[49] UNICEF, on the other hand, has estimated that number to be 1.2 million,[50] while the United Nations has set it at 12.5 million.[51]

Why is there such disparity? Because again, this business is off the radar. It exists in the shadows. Think about it: It's relatively easy to tell if someone is trying to smuggle drugs across the Mexico-U.S. border—they will have the contraband on their person, in their car or somewhere else that it could potentially be discovered. But what if what they're smuggling is a person? A young child? Someone's wife or sister? As was noted by John Miller, director of the State Department's Office to Monitor and Combat Trafficking in Persons, people who are being trafficked do not "stand in line and raise their hands to be counted."[52] And when confronted with nothing more than a car full of people, how would a Border Patrol agent be able to see that anything illegal was going on—especially considering that the people being trafficked often do not even know what is happening to them?

I believe that if anything, the estimates of people trafficked internationally every year—even the larger numbers—are grossly underestimated. There are just too many invisible ways for the practice to be carried out. Throughout the world, there are so many brothels offering underage girls, sweatshops operating behind closed doors, massage parlors offering "unadvertised" services and other forms of slavery that just are not apparent to an untrained eye—or, at least, to an eye that does not want to see it. If it's not right in front of our faces, and it's kept so secret, how can we really know how rampant the problem actually is?

Unfortunately, the statistics on human trafficking into and within the United States are no less confounding. In 2002, the Department of Justice asserted that the indeterminate "U.S. government"[53] estimated 50,000 women and children being trafficked into the country. Then, in a June 2008 report, the State Department said that up to 17,500 people—including men this time—are trafficked into the U.S. each year.[54] What happened to those other 32,500 people? Could trafficking really have decreased that much in just six years?

Sadly, I tend to think not. I also think that these inconsistencies in the assessments of today's slave trade are indicative of just how hard it is to pin this epidemic down—and a sign that the U.S. government needs to put a lot more focus on the issue. Later in this chapter we will take a look at what they are doing about it now, and what they could be doing better.

Part of the current problem is that in the United States, most people are under the impression that slavery died with the Emancipation Proclamation, but that could not be further from the truth. Human trafficking within and into this country is a business that is on its way to financially outperforming drug and weapons trafficking, according to the Department of Homeland Security.[55] In 2004, a group called Free the Slaves and The Human Rights Center of the University of California at Berkeley estimated that over 10,000 people were living in the United States as indentured servants,[56] working mostly in homes (as domestic helpers), restaurants and hotels, the agricultural industry and factories. However, the number-one "job" held by modern-day slaves in the United States was, by far, prostitution.[57] The U.S. is, in fact, one of the top three "destination countries" in the area of sex trafficking, along with Japan and Australia.[58]

The women and girls who are trafficked into the U.S. specifically for use in the sex trade are largely from Southeast Asia, the former Soviet Union and South America, and can be found most often in California, New York, Texas and Las Vegas[59]—which are, coincidentally or not, also areas of high concentration for illegal immigrants. Often, these women and children are brought into the country illegally; they are flown into Canada or Mexico and then walked or driven to California with no legal documentation. Sometimes, they fly directly to their destinations in the U.S. and get through customs with fake passports and visas.[60]

Once the women are in, they are taken to what they believe will be their new jobs—the lucrative career offers that lured them to the U.S. in the first place. However, what they usually find are massage parlors, apartments or other hovels in which they are literally locked up, alone or in groups, and forced to perform sex acts with countless men on a daily basis. Their travel documents and identification are confiscated, so that if they do escape, they will be powerless—they will be nobodies. They do not get paid for this exploitation; their "owners" keep all their profits as reimbursement for their travel or living expenses, the constantly changing totals of which guarantee that they will never be paid off.[61]

But this sort of horror does not just happen to people who are brought here from other countries. In the U.S., there's a growing problem with trafficking between states as well, particularly of minors. In 2001, the University of Pennsylvania released a report estimating that 293,000 underage Americans, mostly kids who had run away from or been abandoned by their families, were at risk of "becoming victims of commercial sexual exploitation,"[62] including trafficking, as early as age twelve for girls and age eleven for boys and transgender youth.[63]

Frighteningly, there are also cases in which average young people, from what we would consider good families and good homes, are abducted and forced into prostitution. An ABC News report detailed the story of a fifteen-year-old girl who was taken right from her own driveway by sex traffickers—unbelievably, with the help of one of her friends. She was kept locked up in an apartment twenty-five miles from her home, where she was drugged and repeatedly raped by both her captors and men who paid them for access to her. It was later learned that the traffickers had put an ad on the Internet, offering her for sale, and there were many takers. She was constantly physically abused and psychologically debased, and was told that if she tried to escape, her kidnappers would harm her family. After more than forty days, the police finally found her—tied up and shoved into a drawer beneath a bed, but at least alive.[64]

Sometimes, the abduction is not so brutal. The same ABC report discussed another girl, nineteen years old, who worked in a mall in Phoenix, Arizona, and was conned by a customer who posed as a modeling agent—and ended up selling her into prostitution. Once he lured her to California with the promise of a photo shoot, he kidnapped her and kept moving her from place to place, putting ads on the Internet to let potential "clients" know where she would be. She only escaped when the trafficker got too greedy and put her out on the street, unsupervised, to turn tricks.[65]

So the conclusion we can draw here is that an illegal sex trade is alive and well in the United States of America. While, as we already saw, many of its victims are drawn from within the country itself, we must look, again, at our relationship with Latin America when it comes to this issue. Why?

Because the figures support it. Let's start with the fact that tens of millions of Latin American women support themselves and their families via prostitution.[66] And, further, that advocacy groups have repeatedly cited Guatemala, El Salvador, Honduras, Nicaragua and Costa Rica as major offenders when it comes to sex trafficking, child prostitution and the "sex tourism" trade,[67] wherein men from other countries travel there for the sole purpose of paying for sex with minors. Sex tourism is also common in Mexico, especially along its border with the United States—particularly in Tijuana, near San Diego, California, and Ciudad Juarez, close to El Paso, Texas.[68]

Now let's look at the fact that at current estimate, 38 million people of Latin American descent live within the U.S., making them our largest ethnic minority. Whether they come here legally or illegally, they bring with them their own cultures, customs and ethics—which often includes the long-fabled idea of *machismo*, an ideology in which men hold free reign to "completely dominate"[69] their wives, daughters and sisters. Far from a fairy tale, it is this attitude—which is streaming into America along with the immigrants and not being phased out through assimilation—that makes this population so susceptible to sex trafficking. Add to that the fact that so many Hispanics in the U.S. come from countries where prostitution is legal (or at least ignored by local officials, even when it involves children) and you've got a real recipe for disaster on your hands.

Given these facts, as Hispanics continue to populate more areas in the U.S., undoubtedly we will see the sex trafficking trend rise even further. Already, Latino brothels are popping up around the country, in such widespread areas as the suburbs of Washington, D.C.,[70] Ohio,[71] Boston,[72] North Carolina[73] and Minneapolis.[74] Referred to as "social clubs"[75] (though not all Latino social clubs are brothels), they sometimes offer gambling and alcohol in order to bring in customers,[76] in addition to a standard $30 for fifteen minutes fee.[77] Often, they are run by interstate prostitution rings. A raid on the D.C.-suburb brothels in Maryland and Virginia, for example, found that they were populated mostly by women from the New York area who had been promised good money if they were willing to travel there for "work."

Aside from the foothold these sex traffickers are gaining within the U.S., there is still the problem of the passage of women and children across our border with Mexico. A byproduct of Mexico's criminal underworld, Mexican sex traffickers often victimize people of their own country as well as other Central Americans who want a "better life" or to make money to send home to their families, and so turn to smugglers to get them into the U.S., agreeing to work, once they get here, until their debt to the smugglers is paid.

This is what happened to three unsuspecting, underage girls from Mexico in 2007. In a piece in the *San Antonio Express-News*, reporter Guillermo Contreras wrote about how these girls were smuggled into the United States from Mexico by three women, also Hispanic but living in the U.S. at the time. The women promised the girls that they would make big money in Texas as escorts—without any expectations of sex.

Once the girls were in the San Antonio area, however, they were groomed with English lessons and new clothing, and then were sold to a man called "Boss" for $3,000 a piece (even though, it's been said, a person can be bought for a mere $90 in Texas[78]). He told them that they would be working in his prostitution ring for five years to pay off their smuggling debts. For their efforts, the three female smugglers were charged with sex trafficking of children in San Antonio's first case under a federal law targeting human trafficking and slavery—that had been passed seven years earlier.[79]

So we have the laws here to deal with this sort of thing (even if they aren't being enforced as much as we'd like them to be). What, then, is being done on the other side of the border? Mexico is, essentially, a hub for sex trafficking between and among itself, other Central and South American countries and the U.S. And what is its government doing to combat this scourge? Well, they've enacted anti-trafficking laws with some strict enough penalties, including fines and imprisonment. The problem? A June 2008 report by the U.S. State Department noted that since June 2007, there had only been seven federal arrests for sex trafficking, and no federal convictions or punishments.[80]

However, there have been efforts on the state level to combat sex trafficking—a necessity since the federal government generally only gets involved in cases of organized crime or international trafficking. The problem here is that as of April 2008, only five Mexican states had enacted "comprehensive anti-trafficking laws."[81] Good for them; bad for the other twenty-six states and Mexico City, the country's capital and a federal district.

This information comes from the State Department's annual Trafficking in Persons Report, wherein they review what countries around the world are doing to combat human trafficking and then categorize the countries into one of three tiers, much the same as they do with drug trafficking nations. In this case, tier one countries are the best—the ones who are fully compliant with the U.S.'s Trafficking Victims Protection Act of 2000. Tier two countries have shown that they are making good faith efforts at least to meet the law's minimum requirements. Governments that are essentially doing nothing, and letting human traffickers run rampant through their countries, are placed at the bottom, in tier three.[82]

For further distinction, this State Department report also has a tier two "watch list" category that gives special notice to any nations that meet the following criteria:

1. They are in tier one this year but were in tier two last year.
2. They are in tier two this year but were in tier three last year.
3. They are currently in tier two but have a significant amount of severe trafficking victims, cannot provide proof of increased efforts to curb severe trafficking, or have only made it into tier two based on assurances that they will take greater efforts in the future.[83]

While the United States is strangely missing from these rankings, even stranger is that in the 2008 Trafficking in Persons (TIP) Report, Mexico is in tier two, and not even on the watch list. I say it's strange because when you read the country's abstract within the report, it doesn't sound as though they've really earned the right to be so highly classified—especially considering that they *were* on the watch list for the last three years.[84] The TIP report even clearly states: "The Government of Mexico does not fully comply with the minimum standards for the elimination of trafficking,"[85] though it does add that it is "making significant efforts to do so."[86] Since when does effort rate a passing grade? If we do not require real results before moving a nation up to a better tier, then what incentive to change is there for the countries that do not meet the minimum requirements?

So, how has Mexico moved from the tier two watch list when they still do not meet the minimum standards? Let's see. By enacting federal legislation that is rarely enforced. By depending on foreign organizations to deal with their own trafficking victims. By doing nothing to identify and offer help to populations that are at risk of being trafficked.[87] I could go on and on, but the State Department's report already does that. It does list efforts that Mexico's government has undertaken to combat trafficking, but the list of things it *hasn't* done is decidedly longer. Whatever they're doing, it simply, in my opinion, is not enough. Mexico's failure to meet the State Department's standards remains the same today as it was three years ago, and yet they continue to move up the tiers. This shows that the rankings are, at best, inconsistent.

So if Mexico is not going to try to combat their problem with human trafficking, what can we do about it on this side of the border? What can we do to make this country less attractive to human traffickers who bring their "goods" in from or through Mexico? Just as with drug trafficking and illegal immigration, this is an uphill battle, to say the least. Some people—and that includes some of us Americans—will always be evil. There will always be people who think it's okay to make their money by using and abusing other human beings. And, on the other side of the equation, there will always be people who will pay to do the same. It's disgusting, sick and depressing, and there's no solution to it in sight.

But still, we can't just sit by and let it happen. A knee-jerk reaction to the situation would be to throw more money at it—or, take money away from it, which we already supposedly do. Under current guidelines, the U.S. can oppose and even withhold non-humanitarian and non-trade-related foreign aid, from international financial institutions such as the International Monetary Fund and the World Bank, for countries that fail to achieve at least tier-two status. However, it is the prerogative of our president to waive all sanctions when considering national interests.

Still, it would seem that the potential cost to countries that fail to substantively participate in countering trafficking in persons should induce them to do so. Yet, it does not. Why? Because the foreign aid exceptions cited in the previous paragraph brief well, but they are not real deterrents to human trafficking and do not really serve to enforce the U.S.' trafficking in person's policy. Given the broad definition of "non-humanitarian and non-trade-related foreign aid," the only thing that really would be withheld is military aid. And this makes our whole policy rather hollow because most countries are not dependent on the U.S. for military aid.

If we really want to get serious about wiping out the slave trade scourge—with an emphasis on eradicating sex trafficking, which is just an abomination—then there are three policy measures that we should implement:

1. If a country "does not fully comply with the minimum standards for the elimination of slave trafficking,"[88] that country cannot attain a rating higher than tier three.
2. Countries with a tier three designation do not qualify for any foreign aid—no waivers, no exceptions and no executive prerogative based on "national interests."
3. We must gain control of our border with Mexico to deny the cross-border trafficking of persons.

Yes, once again, there is an urgent need for the U.S. to really take a good, hard look at its border with Mexico, and who and what is coming across it. If we're not going to stop human trafficking (or drug trafficking, or illegal immigration) through law enforcement, economic incentives or governmental pressure, then our only remaining option is to cut off its supply route. It may seem simplistic, but think about it: If the traffickers cannot get into the country, how can they do their business here?

If there has ever been a good argument for the U.S. to close its 2,000-mile-long border with Mexico, this is it. Lives could literally depend on it—the lives of the innocent women, children and men who are brought here through that border and forced into situations that they could not have imagined in their worst nightmares. Securing that border, making it impervious to anyone who does not have a legitimate reason to get in here, will not, of course, put an end to human trafficking and the illegal, forced sex trade it supports. But at least it will be a step in the right direction.

PART II
THE RULE OF LAW

Chapter Seven

Constitutional Interpretation

Many people assume that the Founding Fathers deliberately wrote the Constitution in such a convoluted way that only they and a select few others could understand and interpret its true meaning. However, that isn't true. Through designated representatives, the Constitution of the United States was written by the people, for the people; I don't think that its authors meant for us not to understand it.

So, how are we supposed to interpret the Constitution? There are, primarily, three accepted methodologies.

First is textualism, an approach that disregards any attempt at trying to ascertain the intent of the authors and interprets meanings strictly, based solely on the words used in the constitutional text. Second is originalism, a method in which the person doing the interpretation takes into account the intent of those who wrote the document when there are questions as to the breadth and scope of a specific concept. Judge Robert Bork refers to originalism as "original understanding."[89] I highly recommend his book *The Tempting of America: The Political Seduction of the Law.*

The last methodology is non-originalism, in which the reader is free to interpret the Constitution in any way he sees fit. This means that non-originalists *may* consider the intent of the Founders, but they do not *have to* do so. They are free to look to "all potentially relevant sources, including, history and tradition, logic, natural law, moral philosophy, political theory, and social policy."[90]

Now, which methodology seems to make the most sense?

I cannot concur with textualism because it is the nature of our language that words have different meanings depending on their usage, and so they must be placed in their proper context before their meanings are interpreted.

I cannot agree with the non-originalist approach for much the same reason, and because it allows the decision-maker to consult other sources. This should be a warning flag. The U.S. Constitution is meant to be the supreme law of the land—not a piece of writing that can be interpreted subjectively based on each individual's opinions and experiences. The fact that non-originalism allows interpreters to consider political theory and social policy, rather than merely the Constitution itself, is egregious *and* extremely dangerous because it removes the moorings of interpretation from the writing as well as the intent of those who wrote it. In other words, non-originalism makes the U.S. Constitution useless—a moot document. And that, obviously, will never work.

But still, we must have an effective method of reading—and enforcing—the Constitution. And in looking for that we need to ask what point of reference judges use when deciding issues of constitutional law. What is the standard employed when they interpret constitutional issues? There has to be one; if there's no established standard by which all points of law are interpreted, then there's no real foundation to our nation's governmental systems. And if that's the case, then relativism and chaos become the practical standard by default. Fortunately, I don't think that we've slipped that far quite yet.

So, what is our point of reference? It is, of course, our Constitution itself, as it was molded, shaped and framed by our Founding Fathers—that, and only that. When making decisions, judges must follow the word of the law, as it is laid out in our Constitution; it is absolutely not their purview to consider the potential political and social effects of their actions and let them affect the decisions they make. The responsibility to consider such concerns falls to the legislative branch of government.

James Madison gave us some insight into performing legal construction when he wrote, in "The Federalist No. 40":

> There are two rules of construction dictated by plain reason, as well as founded on legal axioms. The one is that every part of the expression ought to be made to conspire to some common end. The other is that where the several parts cannot be made to coincide, the less important should give way to the more important part; the means should be sacrificed to the end, rather than the end to the means.[91]

Madison likely went through this exercise because so many people were apprehensive about what powers the federal government would hold in comparison to the powers that would remain with the various states. Remember that at that time in U.S. history, the Union was a group of independent sovereign states held together rather loosely under the Articles of Confederation. In "The Federalist No. 39," Madison went on to declare that each state that ratified the Constitution would be an independent body, bound only by its voluntary agreement to abide by the document. "In this relation, then," he concluded, "the new Constitution will, if established, be *a federal* and not *a national* constitution."[92] This was an important point for many, because the majority of people in the U.S. did not desire a strong, centralized federal government—easy to understand given the monarchy of England.

In his essay "The Federalist No. 75," Alexander Hamilton noted, "The essence of the legislative authority is to enact laws, or in other words to prescribe rules for the regulation of society."[93] Because of the legislators' proximity to the people they were elected to serve, it was up to the various state legislatures to set down rules that governed their respective states. In fact, the Founders were so serious about representation from the individual states that they prescribed, in the Constitution, that state lawmakers—not the general population of each state—were to elect their respective senators, thus ensuring proper representation of each state in the Senate. This approach also encouraged U.S. Senators to stay attached to their states and constituencies.

So the United States was to be a united country composed of sovereign states that determined the vast majority of their own internal laws and regulations. It was never the intent of the Founders that we have the same rules in every state because that would have made state borders meaningless; the Union would have existed as one large state. And that would have changed the very nature of the country we live in.

After reading *The Federalist Papers*, which included Madison's essay, I concluded that there was apprehension in the states about how much power would be vested in the federal government versus how much would stay with the states. Alexander Hamilton, James Madison and John Jay all devoted considerable attention to the idea that the federal government would only retain such powers as were commensurate with its ability to respond to the exigencies of the Union—in other words, the federal government's powers were to remain very limited and all other powers were to remain with the states.

But still, the states had their fears and in order to allay them, Madison took some time to explain that the Constitution had to be read literally, without taking words, phrases or clauses out of context, because this could, as we have seen many times within the last seventy-five years, lead to what we commonly refer to as "legislation from the bench"—judges' decrees that have absolutely no constitutional footing, and would have absolutely no chance of becoming law through our representative republic.

The Founders were so concerned about this potential abuse of power by the judiciary that they put safeguards in place to prevent such occurrences. An example of this is Article III, Section 2, which states, "…the Supreme Court shall have appellate jurisdiction, both as to Law and Fact, with such exceptions, and Regulations as the Congress shall make."[94]

Additional safeguards were embedded in the checks and balances between our three branches of government. For example, the judiciary does not have the power to enforce its opinions and the legislature can deny funds to the judiciary through the appropriations process.

You may have started to notice a trend here: The people, through their representatives, have the bulk of the power. Majority rule, consistent with the U.S. Constitution, is an interesting concept. However, with tyrannical courts and self-serving political agendas, the needs and desires of the majority are often thwarted.

But let's get back to the issue of interpreting the Constitution. Since our Founding Fathers based their ideas on not only the needs and wants of the people but on a set of standards and policies manifested in the rule of law that would help the collective nation to thrive for centuries to come, why shouldn't we consider their intent when interpreting the U.S. Constitution? I believe that we should, and that the only valid interpretation of the document comes from doing so. This means that only an *originalist* approach to Constitutional law is valid. In taking into account the true and actual intent of the Constitution itself, it is the only methodology capable of ensuring the preservation of the rights and liberties of the people and safeguarding them against big government.

Still, much of what we regard as the law of the land today was not framed by the Founders but is the product of the modern legal process; the rulings have only been in place since the activism of the New Deal Court and the Warren Court. This includes legalized abortion, requiring states to educate illegal immigrants in public schools, and the "establishment clause" cases touting the separation of church and state.

It also includes many questions that can be raised about United States citizenship, and how it pertains to the growing illegal immigrant population within our country's borders—or, at least, their offspring. It's usually assumed that if you are born in the United States, no matter the circumstances, you have the right to U.S. citizenship. But this is not the case; it is just what we have been led to believe by a few select judges' opinions, even though they did not apply our law as it was originally intended. If you ask me, that's an absolute abuse of power.

What does the Constitution have to say about it? Let's consider the text of the Fourteenth Amendment, which states:

> Section 1. All persons born or naturalized in the United States, and subject to the jurisdiction thereof, are citizens of the United States and of the State wherein they reside. No State shall make or enforce any law which shall abridge the privileges or immunities of citizens of the United States; nor shall any State deprive any person of life, liberty, or property without due process of law; nor deny to any person within its jurisdiction the equal protection of the laws.[95]

From this, can we readily conclude that citizenship is guaranteed to the children of illegal immigrants when they are born on U.S. soil? Perhaps, on first reading. But I would consider it a prudent endeavor to research and consider the intent of the author of this section—Senator Jacob Howard. This is what he had to say regarding the passage's meaning:

> Every person born within the limits of the United States, and subject to their jurisdiction, is by virtue of natural law and national law a citizen of the United States. This will not, of course, include persons born in the United States who are foreigners, aliens, who belong to the families of ambassadors or foreign ministers accredited to the government of the United States, but will include all every other class of persons.[96]

Since Senator Howard co-wrote this amendment, it is safe to say that he fully realized what it meant—and what it was intended to do. Here, he clearly stated that the Fourteenth Amendment was never intended to apply to foreigners or aliens, much less illegal aliens.

To clarify the purpose of the Fourteenth Amendment even further, Judge Robert Bork put it in its historical context. He stated, "The fourteenth amendment was adopted shortly after the Civil War, and all commentators are agreed that its primary purpose was the protection of the recently freed slaves... [and] the desire to protect blacks from discriminatory laws and law enforcement."[97]

In other words, it was intended to solve a dilemma with regard to the disposition of the former slaves residing within our country, not—as Senator Howard clearly stated—to grant citizenship to the children of foreigners or aliens, including illegal aliens. That was what the Founding Fathers intended, and thus, that is what we must honor and uphold today.

Chapter Eight

Tyranny

When all government, domestic and foreign, in little as in great things, shall be drawn to Washington as the center of power, it will render powerless the checks provided of one government on another, all will become as venal and oppressive as the government from which we separated.
—President Thomas Jefferson

I studied constitutional law at the United States Military Academy and continued my study of the Constitution for many years after graduating from West Point. I have wrestled with what I have concluded to be the correct manner for interpreting the Constitution because several Supreme Court opinions differ from what I've concluded—as do other constitutional scholars, such as Judges Bork and Napolitano. Such dissent can be troubling for those of us who care about truth and the preservation of our rights and liberties, and what power "we the people" have to enact laws.

So often during my research, it has appeared to me that the federal government, including the federal courts, forces its citizens to bend to its will rather than follow the Constitution to the letter—a phenomenon that is very apparent in the realm of illegal immigration. For example, let's take a look at some of the financial baggage we taxpayers have been saddled with in order to educate non-English-speaking children. According to the Texas Education Agency, there are approximately 600,000 non-English-speaking students in the Texas education system. This leads to an additional estimated $1.03 billion that has to be budgeted in per year—a figure that does not even include costs related to traditional classroom education. These are dollars that Texas is spending over and above what is considered necessary to educate the legal citizens of Texas.[98]

Why are so many non-English-speaking, school-age children enrolled in Texas schools? I'm sure that some live here legally, and that's fine. However, I'm going to assume that many are illegal immigrant children. Let us assume a couple of figures, so we can derive an estimated cost that Texans incur in order to provide education to illegal immigrants. At present, the State of Texas pays about $10,000 per student *per annum* in its public school system. Since the Texas Education Agency used the figure of 600,000 non-English-speaking children in the state's school system, let's do the math to determine how much that costs Texas each year:

600,000 x $10,000 = $6 billion

Something that I consider very interesting is that Texas addressed the problem of illegal immigrant children in its schools many years ago, only to have its efforts overridden by an activist Supreme Court. In *Plyler v. Doe* (1982), the U.S. Supreme Court decided, in a 5-4 vote, that the State of Texas was required to educate illegal immigrants in its public school system.

The holding of the U.S. Supreme Court was:

> A Texas statute which withholds from local school districts any state funds for the education of children who are not "legally admitted" into the United States, and which authorizes local school districts to deny enrollment to such children, violates the Equal Protection Clause of the Fourteenth Amendment.[99]

In laymen's terms, the State of Texas has to educate people who are not legal citizens of the United States. At first glance, does this seem a bit odd to you?

When a case is brought before the U.S. Supreme Court, what are the options that are available to the court? One is to hear the case and render a decision based on its constitutional merits. This is appropriate as fulfillment of the court's accepted judicial review function—which is not in the Constitution, but seems to be a prudent check on a legislative or executive action that may be infringing on the Constitution.

The other option is for the court to state that the Constitution is "silent" on the question before the court. In other words, that since the question is not a constitutional matter, it is not a matter for the court to consider.

Either one of these is acceptable and in keeping with the idea of the Constitution as the law of the land—the document by which we all are ruled. However, sometimes, the U.S. Supreme Court oversteps its bounds and creates its own third option: It renders a decision on a matter that clearly has no constitutional footing. What is the recourse of the legislature when this happens?

Typically, the legislature just says, "Oh, well, we tried, but the court said that our law was unconstitutional." And to that, I say, "What a bunch of cowards." How about getting some intestinal fortitude and doing what's right and just instead? How about following the Constitution as it's meant to be enforced instead of using the courts for cover so you don't have to take the rap for an abysmal failure in the eyes of your constituents? It's unbelievable to me that things like this actually happen.

The way things are now, the courts are expected to be a check on the legislative and executive branches—and yet, there seem to be extremely few checks on the courts. Some may argue that the only check on the courts is provided for through the election of the president, who can choose not to enforce court opinions or to take action through his power to appoint Supreme Court and other federal judges. That is one option. But I believe that there are other means of recourse when the courts, either state or federal, overreach their constitutional authority.

In fact, our Constitution provides for it. The words of our Founding Fathers allow the legislature to deny funding to the judicial branch, except for pay; it can also remove the court's jurisdiction on particular matters (as can state legislatures) and choose to ignore the courts altogether. These are powerful, constitutionally driven tools that can be used to keep our nation's highest arbiters of law in line and in check, yet when do we ever hear about them in use? We often hear about courts challenging legislative and executive actions, but rarely the other way around, despite the fact that Article III, Section 2 of the U.S. Constitution allows for such "exceptions."

For some reason, people don't like this idea. There seems to be an image of our Supreme Court as the be all, end all, the last word in the country, untouchable to anyone who may object. "We are a nation of laws!" many people cry in the face of this dilemma, as if challenging our courts' decisions would somehow bring about anarchy.

My problem with that retort is that it's similar to the catchall, leftist cry of racism whenever anyone speaks out against Obama on any number of his stupid policy proposals. Racism has nothing to do with the situation. The guy is a Socialist, that's the problem. But whenever there is opposition to his beliefs, his supporters cry "racism!" and just expect the matter to be dropped—the same as those who say that it's not right to challenge our highest court's decisions. It's as if they think their simple, unsupported "argument" holds any water.

The way I see it, challenging court decisions is not only right, it's necessary; however, it's also difficult. The problem starts with the decisions themselves, which are too often almost impossible for any layperson to understand. I wasn't in law school very long, but in that time I prepared an enormous number of case briefs and what I figured out very early on was that there was, more often than not, no rhyme or reason in the way court opinions were structured. When there was a constitutional question before the court, it would seem appropriate for the court to state what it was and then specifically argue how the actions of a certain legislature differed from the Constitution. However, the opinions were not written this way, and anyone looking at them would have to dig and dig into the morass of often flowery and irrelevant verbiage to unearth the cogent information. They would also have to draw numerous inferences as to what the court's words actually meant, and then try to draw their own conclusions. Who does this confusion serve? Certainly not the people of the United States.

So, let me offer a recommendation on how we *can* better serve the people: We should establish a standard format for all court opinions, so that everybody can understand how the court arrived at its decision. Lawyers will hate this because it will take the murkiness out of the opinions and, therefore, empower average citizens to know what's going on—instead of the reverse, which is the prevalent situation now.

To create a more understandable opinion, first the court should briefly state what is at issue. Second, it should cite all constitutional points of law that have relevance to the question at hand. Third, it should provide adequate analysis to demonstrate, using originalism to interpret the Constitution, and not precedent, how the points of law under scrutiny are either in keeping with the Constitution or at variance with it. And, lastly, if the law under consideration is at odds with the Constitution, the court will be at liberty to offer recommendations as to how to bring the law into compliance with the Constitution.

The next step would be for the legislative branch to review the opinion of the court. Depending on the merits of the court's arguments, the legislature could either agree or disagree with the court's opinion. It would also be up to the executive branch as to whether to enforce the opinion or not. Our executives and legislatures at the state and federal levels are asleep at the wheel when it comes to their constitutional authority as it pertains to the courts. Rewind to the leftist argument of "we are a nation of laws."

The problem that exists today is that there is no recourse for the legislature when an activist court issues an opinion that is not justified in the law. It is baffling to me that something that is not based on the law can somehow become "the law of the land." If it is not *from* the law, then how can it *become* law? It cannot, and it is therefore null and void, and the legislative branch should treat the court's opinion accordingly. After all, it is a legislative prerogative to write law—not a court's prerogative. And yet, it takes only five out of nine justices to overturn the decisions of 535 members of Congress or the legislatures of individual states.

With all that said, let us look at the Supreme Court's opinion in *Plyler v. Doe*, the aforementioned case in which the U.S. Supreme Court ruled that Texas had to allow illegal immigrants into its public schools.

At first glance, the arguments and justifications put forth in the majority opinion are not very convincing. One would think that the way to argue would be to begin with the point of law, and then to proceed forward to demonstrate how the action taken by Texas deviated from that point of law. However, the majority opinion did not make good use of our laws, as outlined in our Constitution, to make the case for its final opinion.

First, they stated that the actions of Texas violated the Equal Protection Clause of the Fourteenth Amendment. At this point, one would assume that the argument would take shape and justify, through the employment of legal definitions, facts and analysis, its conclusion as to how exactly Texas violated the clause as it applied to non-United States citizens.

The Court said that an alien is a "'person' in any ordinary sense of that term."[100] This references the "all persons" terminology used in the Fourteenth Amendment and, without analysis that relies on original understanding of these words, the judges' comment would be accurate. But when you shine the light of intent on the words "all persons," we know that the amendment's authors did not mean to include aliens. How can anybody totally disregard cogent facts that are available when making a decision? Remember, it was never the intent of the Founders for the people to be governed by a judicial oligarchy.

In *Plyler v. Doe*, the justices also argued another part of the conjunctive sentence containing the words "all persons" that uses the words "within its jurisdiction." I agree that any person who is within the sovereign borders of the United States and its territories comes under the jurisdiction thereof, but there is a difference between what actions should be taken when dealing with a U.S. citizen and a non-U.S. citizen. For example, do illegal immigrants automatically benefit from the privileges and immunities clause of our Constitution because they are within the jurisdiction of our country? The answer is "no." Do all citizens enjoy the same privileges and immunities? The answer is "yes."

What illegal immigrants should be receiving is due process of our immigration laws. When we talk about the due process clause, we are merely affirming that all citizens of the U.S. will receive the same legal consideration and treatment from the government. This is only fair and is meant to prevent abuses by an over-reaching government. It is also an example of how our Constitution protects the rights of the minority—but not illegal immigrants because they are not citizens and therefore have no rights as defined by our Constitution. We can treat them with dignity and respect, but we must ensure that illegal immigrants receive the due process of law that applies to them.

Now, did the *Plyler v. Doe* opinion entertain any of these ideas? No, it did not. Instead, the justices explained the societal effects on people who do not have adequate education, and how the children—the liberals love to make everything about "the children"—are "a discrete class...not accountable for their disabling status."[101] However, it is absolutely not the prerogative of judges to consider the societal effects of their opinions. Their charter is to identify the legal standard (point of law), assess whether or not there is deviation from that legal standard, and when they find a deviation, to state that fact. In this case, the majority of the justices took it upon themselves to invalidate an action taken by the legislature of the State of Texas because they did not agree with what the state decided to do about its illegal immigrant children. And they did this even though it is the prerogative of the legislatures to decide societal matters. As long as their actions are constitutional, the courts have absolutely no authority to change legislative actions.

This is the clincher in Justice Brennan's majority opinion of the court that "the illegal alien of today may well be the legal alien tomorrow."[102] Put it that way, I understand why the court arrived at its opinion. But where is the discussion of the law in all of this rhetoric? If the record of Senator Howard's comments had instructed that the words "all persons," in regard to who deserved the amendment's protections, were to include aliens, I would have to agree with the court. However, his comments revealed that the exact opposite is the case, and so I have to disagree with Justice Brennan who, in essence, said that there is no way to construct the Fourteenth Amendment to mean anything other than what the majority of the court says it means. That is not a valid argument. It is nothing more than a comment that has no support in historical fact.

Justice Burger wrote the dissenting opinion of the court, which included Justices White, Rehnquist and O'Connor as well. To paraphrase the minority opinion, there was agreement that it would not be advisable to create an illiterate segment of society. However, they asserted that the Court has no constitutional authority to strike down laws because they may not meet with desirable societal policy.

Justice Burger went on to say,

> We trespass on the assigned function of the political branches [i.e., the Texas legislature] under our structure of limited and separated powers when we assume a policymaking role as the Court does today… [I]t is not the function of the judiciary to provide "effective leadership" simply because the political branches of government fail to do so.[103]

I find it particularly interesting that Justice Burger went on to say that:

> The Court employs, and in my view abuses, the Fourteenth Amendment in an effort to become an omnipotent and omniscient problem solver. That the motives are noble and compassionate does not alter the fact that the Court distorts our constitutional function to make amends for the defaults of others.[104]

Court opinions are not supposed to be the trump cards with which the courts supersede the constitutional actions that our elected legislators take to enact laws.

Chapter Nine

Posse Comitatus

As we continue to lay the foundation before we proceed to the specifics of what we need to do to solve our border defense dilemma, let me address posse *comitatus* and the Posse Comitatus Act (PCA). This is an important legal concept with regard to securing our nation's borders and enforcing our laws.

First, the meaning of *posse comitatus*: "the power of the sheriff to call upon any able-bodied adult men (and presumably women) in the county to assist him in apprehending a criminal."[105] We've seen the exercise of *posse comitatus* in the news recently with the Arizona sheriff, Joe Arpaio, as he endeavors to do what is right for the people he serves in Maricopa County. He has organized modern sheriff posses to assist his department in illegal immigration control. I applaud Sheriff Arpaio because he is a true leader and a clear example of what we should be doing across our entire country to repulse this invasion from our southern border.

The Posse Comitatus Act, according to *Black's Law Dictionary*, "is a federal law that, with few exceptions, prohibits the Army and the Air Force from directly participating in civilian law-enforcement operations, such as making arrests, conducting searches, or seizing evidence."[106]

The PCA was a proposal, primarily from Southern legislators, to end what they thought to be military abuses of their citizens during Reconstruction in the South from 1865–1877, when federal soldiers were deployed there to maintain law and order. The PCA was passed in 1878 to prevent federal troops from supervising elections and performing law enforcement activity within the United States itself.

However, the PCA states that there are certain exceptions to the prohibitions set forth in the act, such as the war on drugs or whenever there is rebellion or anticipated rebellion within the United States. Given that, in our particular situation, I conclude that the Congress has every power to authorize the use of the military in defending our country's borders. The threats this unsecured passage poses to our very livelihoods are many and varied. And preventing the entry of non-U.S. citizens, terrorists and drug traffickers into our country does not conflict with the PCA.

In fact, I am very much in favor of using the military on the border and not just the National Guard—and not just as backup to law enforcement, either. The fact that the president has limited the role of National Guard on our southern border so that it is subservient to the U.S. Border Patrol is ridiculous. The military is there only to observe illegal immigrant entry, report it to the Border Patrol, and support agents in their enforcement efforts. But what kind of support can they be if they are not allowed to *do* anything? We need a strong military presence on our southern border with full authority and mandate to secure our nation from this *very real* invasion from Mexico and other countries to the south.

In 2006, on national television, President Bush stated that we will not "militarize the southern border" and that "Mexico is our neighbor, and our friend."[107] I thought I agreed with him until I did some research, and then I concluded that the opposite is indeed the case.

For all of the reasons I have cited already, I conclude that Mexico is not our friend. Mexico will continue unabated what it has been doing to us for the last several decades unless we, the American people, stand up for what we want as citizens of this great nation. We must quit the never-ending appeasement of those who are friendly neither to us nor to the values and traditions that we hold dear to our hearts.

In the military, there is a policy of sharing the bottom line upfront when giving a briefing. It's called "BLUF." I will use the same method here. The bottom line, as I see it, is that we Americans are the laughing stock of many countries around the world as a result of some of our imbecilic policies on border security and immigration.

Recently, I was talking to two Portuguese, legal immigrants to the United States. Their names were Walter and Kim. When I met them, Walter wore an American flag lapel pin. You've gotta love that—and I can tell you that I sincerely do.

They were both here working toward their U.S. citizenship, and they were great guys who would be a real benefit to this wonderful country of ours. Kim even offered to work as a volunteer on my campaign for the state legislature and apologized for the fact that he would not be able to vote for me because he was not naturalized yet.

Walter had been working toward his citizenship for thirteen years at that point, and Kim had been doing the same for almost as long. Of their many comments to me, one in particular really sticks in my mind: that the United States is the only country in the world where services offered to illegal immigrants are even given in their language. At that point, they both chuckled a bit awkwardly because we all knew that it was not really all that hilarious.

In my travels through Eastern Europe I discovered that people in that region were perplexed over the notion that we Americans welcome, within our borders, certain groups of people who are not all that industrious. They would repeatedly ask, "Why does the United States keep letting people in through the legal immigration process when many of those people are not going to be positive or meaningful contributors to the society?" That was a great question, and I did not know how to answer it. Yes, we are, indeed, a laughing stock around the world for our unsound immigration policies.

The people in Eastern Europe with whom I spoke exposed another interesting point about the education level of many of the people who reside in the former Soviet Union (FSU) countries. Since many of them do not have much, they have turned their efforts toward improvement through schooling. Probably hundreds of thousands of these educated, ambitious people would gladly emigrate to the United States. However, their quota allocation is such that there is really no hope of winning a chance at citizenship through the lottery system that is currently in place.

Let me give you an idea of the immigration numbers authorized by our government. We theoretically allow up to one million legal immigrants into our country each year. Currently, we try to bring in skilled people as roughly sixty percent of our legal immigrants. So, what about that other forty percent? I fail to understand why the United States does not only take the best and brightest of the potential legal immigrants into this country—and *only* the best and brightest.

Is there some unknown reason why we should make way for more unskilled laborers in America? Do we not have enough impoverished and uneducated people who need help? Is there some responsibility that requires America to cater to those who are not going to contribute to our society in a positive way? Is it our responsibility to assist other nations in ridding themselves of those people who are not very productive?

Each and every year, the United States already does more than enough to try to buttress many of the societies around the world through socioeconomic aid in the multi-billion dollar range. As if that were not sufficient, however, it appears to be the opinion of some that the United States must slowly bleed to death in order to save the rest of the world.

So what's the answer? How do we keep our country from self-destructing? Some say that big government is the end-all solution but I don't believe that because government is inherently wasteful and a poor steward of taxpayer dollars. One of our worst breaches is the fact that we continue to send foreign aid to countries fraught with corruption. What happens to these hard-earned taxpayer dollars once they're released to these corrupt nations? It's very simple. Often, the corrupt governments make use of the money for their own gain; very little of it trickles down to the people who are really in need.

However, many private, nonprofit organizations do good jobs of getting real aid to the people who are most in need. So, why don't we simply make better use of those resources instead of always having our government barge in? In addition, our churches are doing outstanding work around the world to help people in need—and they do this because they consider it their Christian duty, not for money or power or prestige. What better group is there for conducting humanitarian aid?

My proposed solution, then, is to help those in need within their own nations rather than absorbing the masses into our own. This, I believe, would make the world a better place to live in overall. And to do this, we will have to start with securing our borders and abandoning the various amnesty proposals floating around out there.

Chapter Ten

Whose Responsibility is Immigration?

The bulk of the enumerated powers vested in the federal government of the United States by our Constitution are in Article I, Section 8. Our Founders' purpose was to limit the power of the federal government by spelling out exactly what was to be a federal responsibility versus the individual states' responsibilities.

For example, it specifically states, "To establish an uniform Rule of Naturalization…"[108] According to *The Federalist Papers*, this was a power believed best left to the federal government because to do otherwise would lend itself to a lack of uniformity in naturalization laws.[109]

Now, let me ask you a question: Does naturalization also mean immigration?

Let us take a moment to compare the definitions of these two words. According to *Black's Law Dictionary*, "naturalization" means "the granting of citizenship to a foreign-born person under statutory authority,"[110] and "immigration" means "the act of entering a country with the intention of settling there permanently."[111]

Is it just me, or is it a fact that these words do not have the same meaning? I believe this to be an important distinction because of what the Constitution states and what Madison had to say on the issue of naturalization.

I have read the Constitution, reviewed *The Federalist Papers* and researched other sources, and I cannot find anything that states that the states do not have the constitutional power, as originally intended by the Founders, to regulate the immigration of people into the respective states. I am referring to people immigrating into the United States, not to other Americans who are choosing where they want to live.

All the Constitution requires is that the standards for naturalization be uniform. I cannot find any constitutional justification that declares that the states have to sit back and do nothing in the event they are invaded by exploiters of our country. Are we just supposed to sit back and keep taking one for the team on this issue? By the way, I would like to know for which team we are taking it. It surely is not the team backed by the citizens of the United States.

Furthermore, in "The Federalist No. 44," James Madison says that "no state shall engage in war unless actually invaded, or in such imminent danger as would not admit of delay."[112] It is clear that we are being invaded and that we—the states—are in imminent danger even though the invasion is subtle and is not readily obvious to all Americans. Can anyone say that our states—especially border states—can make good cases that they have been and are being invaded? I conclude "yes."

Where am I going with this? In order to discuss this perspective, let's take the example of the right of gun ownership as guaranteed by our Constitution's Second Amendment. I have a gun, and I use it for home defense. Uh oh! I may as well confess now that I am a card-carrying, lifetime member of the National Rifle Association (NRA) and the Texas State Rifle Association (TSRA), too.

I realize that law enforcement can only respond to a crisis after a certain amount of time. I do not expect the police to be able to answer my 911 call for assistance immediately when there is a criminal breaking into my house. Consequently, I understand that it is primarily my responsibility to take appropriate precautions to safeguard my home from intrusion—and then personally deal with any criminals who attempt to get in.

Now, I look at the illegal immigrant invasion of the states within the Union in a similar fashion. Just as the police cannot always be there to defend my home immediately against a criminal intrusion, there is ample evidence to support the conclusion that the federal government is not able to protect the states from this illegal invasion—or that it is not willing to do so.

So why do we keep hearing that illegal immigrants are solely a federal problem? Why is it generally assumed that the states have no purview of authority when it comes to protecting themselves? If I were to come home one evening and find a person plundering my belongings, am I just supposed to yield to this wrongdoer? I think not. And our state governments should not be expected to do so in the case of the border invasion.

Why is this happening? One reason is that we have many state-level politicians who are unwilling to provide leadership on this issue—which is at a crisis level in many states. Whatever agendas they had in pursuing statewide public office apparently lacked a selfless concern for the citizens of their states and districts.

Another major concern of the Founders was the prospect of faction in the Union. After all, one of the most compelling arguments for uniting was national defense. In fact, the subject of defense was a significant driver for the U.S. Constitution in the first place. The Founders believed that the only way to address defense adequately was through a centralized power—that the federal government would be expected to raise and equip those forces necessary to provide for the common defense of the states.

All a person needs to do is take some time to read *The Federalist Papers* and it will become very obvious that the Founders were fearful of rebellion, faction and sedition within the country. It was not believed that a confederation could be strong enough to respond to such crises as mentioned above. For example, if there were an Indian attack on Georgia, what was the incentive for New York to rally to Georgia's defense? Why should Georgia have been expected to have to fight alone against an enemy that threatened its sovereignty? A reasonable conclusion is that the concerns of the Founders were legitimate and that it was imperative for the central government to have the power and the means to safeguard the Union.

Let us take these precepts for the Union and fast-forward to the present. We're currently experiencing an outright invasion of our nation that threatens her very sovereignty. It would appear that our situation is desperate, and yet many of our elected politicians take no substantive action in our defense.

Then, when citizens stand up and try to do something about securing our own borders, we are told that we cannot do anything because border security is a federal responsibility.

Do you really think that the Founders intended for the citizenry to sit back and do nothing in the event that the federal authorities did next-to-nothing to secure the nation's borders? The very idea of allowing those who care nothing about our traditions, culture, values and way of life to wage total economic and cultural war on us is unbelievable. Where are the true patriots of old when we need them most?

There are heroes today who are trying to do something because of the government's inaction. One group is known as the Minuteman Project. I am at a total loss as to why our own president would call these patriots "vigilantes."[113] This is another example of trying to throw up a smoke screen because many of our elected politicians are not really doing anything to defend us against the evils that are currently assailing us on many fronts. At the moment, the defense of the homeland is grossly deficient and therefore not viable.

PART III
IMMIGRATION

Chapter Eleven

Seeking Perfection

In a talk in Mexico City, Colin Powell asserted that erecting walls along the U.S.-Mexico border would not solve the illegal immigration problem. He went on to give "proof" of his opinion by stating that the Berlin Wall did not work perfectly and that the wall that the Israelis are putting up is not going to work perfectly either.[114]

I understand that. But who said anything about perfection?

I do not believe that any American honestly thinks that we can keep every single illegal immigrant out with a wall, but the desire for a barrier of some sort is there. After all, isn't it a much better prospect to have only a handful getting into our country each day rather than the thousands who pour over now? Since we elect our representatives, they need to get busy and accomplish this task on behalf of their constituents.

You've got to love what Mr. Powell said in defense of a temporary worker program, too: "We have to find a way for them to live in dignity," he said, "and not in fear."[115]

Now that's a real jewel, isn't it? Whose choice was it for them to come here illegally? And *we're* supposed to make them feel better about it?

I am actually a bit disappointed because I thought Mr. Powell was a little more independent-minded than that. However, he appears to perpetuate the president's talking points without regard for the facts. I conclude that history bears out the fact that the Berlin Wall was a success for the oppressors who used it to keep people locked up within East Germany—very few people ever made it out of the Communist-controlled areas. I also know firsthand that the barrier between the East and the West worked well because I was stationed there. The fact is that we manned it and held the Warsaw Pact at bay for several decades.

As for the Israelis, I conclude that they will man their wall once it is built and gain a higher degree of control over who can enter their country. That's all I'm talking about here—gaining control over our borders. Is this a concept that is that difficult to grasp? I don't think it should be.

Yet for some, I imagine, it still is and that is based on a long history of taking the easy way out, starting with the Immigration Reform and Control Act (IRCA) of 1986—a misleading piece of legislation if ever there was one. I find it telling that almost every time we—the people of the United States—turn around, we are told that something that is obviously true is not actual fact. This situation is the result of misinformation attributable to the power elites and is often facilitated by very willing accomplices: the mass media.

For instance, we keep hearing that the Comprehensive Immigration Reform Act of 2006 was not amnesty because there is no mention of the word "amnesty" in it. However, there is a problem with this argument. As noted by Edwin Meese III, attorney general of the United States under President Ronald Reagan, in an op-ed piece describing the similarities between the IRCA legislation and some of the newer legislation being proposed:

> [T]he 1986 Immigration Reform and Control Act provided amnesty for undocumented immigrants already in the country... Like the amnesty bill of 1986, the current Senate proposal would place those who have resided illegally in the United States on a path to citizenship, provided they meet a similar set of conditions and pay a fine and back taxes.[116]

This relates to what I was talking about before—that there is currently no real and meaningful punishment for those who broke our laws to get into our country. Moreover, his statement confirms that what is being proposed is nothing short of amnesty.

I don't care if Senator John McCain said that Senate Bill 2611, which he supported, does not call for amnesty or that it isn't called "amnesty." So what? Call it "bananas" if you like. It's still what it is—and it *is* amnesty. It's also an absolute non-starter for the American people.

When President George W. Bush spoke to the nation on May 15, 2006, he repeated that he does not support amnesty and that his proposals are "not amnesty."[117] But—and this is a big but—he also said, "We must face the reality that millions of illegal immigrants are already here."[118]

That statement was a blinding flash of the obvious, and it did not change what the majority of the American people want.

Then, the president stated that his plan is not amnesty because such a policy would reward illegal behavior. So what is his solution? To punish all of the lawbreakers by making them go to the end of the line and start from the beginning of the immigration process. This, again, is so much meaningless double-speak, and it amounts to one thing: amnesty.

Let us examine for a moment this immigration process that we are discussing. Where does this process actually begin?

A skilled and educated foreign national who wants to come to the United States has the choice of waiting—often years and perhaps decades—to immigrate legally to the U.S. or coming here on a temporary visa and trying to stay through extensions of that visa. If the latter method fails, then he has the option of overstaying his visa and becoming an illegal immigrant—and then awaiting another offer of amnesty-that-is-not-amnesty.

However, even for those standing in line for U.S. citizenship, it is obvious that their place in line is absolutely not a given. What the president proposes is allowing the illegal immigrants already in our country to go to the end of the line—which is still remaining in the line. In other words, he is proposing to permit them to butt in line ahead of all of the other foreigners who would otherwise be in front of them because those others have been waiting patiently to begin the immigration process legally from their home countries. This means that the legitimate immigrants who are trying to do things right would have to wait at home, while the illegal immigrants continue to live here as they wait at the "back of the line."

In the end, the president's immigration plan is nothing short of amnesty for all of the lawbreakers—with some discriminators thrown in—who made it into this country by whatever illegal means.

The leftists—and I include John McCain in that group—and the internationalists say that the Senate proposal is not amnesty because the lawbreakers have to pay a fine (around $3,000) as well as taxes owed. This doesn't seem to be very much of a penalty for breaking our laws and ultimately obtaining U.S. citizenship. Also, I would really like to know how the federal government plans to figure out how much taxes these illegal workers owe.

Really, this is just so much smoke and mirrors. Many of the illegals paid human smugglers, called *coyotes*, to get them into the country and their fees are much more than any amount we are planning to impose on them. Adding a superficial sum for guaranteed amnesty and citizenship is mighty small compensation for their previous violations of our laws and sovereignty. Keep in mind the fact that many illegal immigrants do not pay taxes and thus, they are better able to build wealth—compared to Americans whose dreams are often stymied because of the tax burden in this country. Consequently, many illegal immigrants are well able to pay such a false penalty.

Therefore, going to the end of the line and paying a fine are nothing more than slick tricks by the big government power elites who think they know better than we do and say that we must allow all of the illegals to remain in this country. The fact is, they are simply attempting to pacify the overwhelming majority of American citizens while ignoring our demands—and lying to us the whole time they are doing it.

Again, the president says that to allow amnesty—which, I have shown, is what he actually proposes—would be a reward of illegal behavior,[119] so we cannot grant it. To that I would say that he is, in fact, rewarding illegal behavior because his plan is truly amnesty. Moreover, if we are to follow his lead on this aspect of immigration reform, we are going to experience a massive influx of illegals trying to get into this country because we will have established a firm precedent for amnesty—as was the case in 1986. It was also contemplated again in 2006, in 2007 and subtly in 2008.

It is well-known that when there are discussions of amnesty for the illegal immigrant population in America, the foreign hopefuls start lining up at the border to take advantage. I've heard at least one congressman state that there may be as many as 25 million foreigners approaching our southern border in anticipation of amnesty. These huge numbers are well worth our consideration. Granting amnesty means rewarding lawlessness with U.S. citizenship and if another round of this is anticipated, many more people will brave the risks and enter our country illegally. They will think that all they have to do is get here and not get caught until amnesty time comes again.

Of course, they may have to wait several years for their citizenship, but the fact remains that each and every one of them will receive it unless they commit some egregious infraction that otherwise disqualifies them from continued consideration—and that's only if they get caught.

The amnesty proposal is nothing short of a sham that attempts to please everybody but the law-abiding citizens of America. "Betrayal" is the word that comes to mind, so shame on you, Mr. President, for turning your back on Americans. When I was out campaigning for a spot in the state legislature, I visited countless homes to listen to and learn from the traditional, die-hard Republicans who vote in the primary. One fact I can convey without equivocation is that many of these active Republican voters are at their wits' ends from trying to understand why their president, in whom they place trust and confidence, is doing nothing about the problems that illegal immigration poses to our country.

The president also proposes a guest worker program. I have no problem with this part of his overall plan—except that it should only apply to potential guest workers, not to those who are already guilty of illegal immigration to the United States. Preferably, it should apply only to guest workers who are educated or have some useful skill, and who have no criminal background or communicable diseases.

The problem is that we must get all other components of our immigration control mechanisms in place before we can even consider allowing guest workers into our country. It only makes sense that before we allow more guest workers to enter, we should secure our borders and account for all the *uninvited* guest workers who are already here. We must do this first because a huge problem with any guest worker program is maintaining accountability of those allowed into this country. We have demonstrated time and again that we are neither proficient nor efficient at keeping track of those we allow to enter our country. And thus, letting more in that we cannot keep track of would only add fuel to the fire.

As for those who are already here—call them illegal immigrants, call them guest workers—they are, often, able to survive here because of local law enforcement that, in essence, allows them to. The local governments of various "sanctuary cities" across the country—including Austin, Dallas, Houston, Los Angeles, New York and San Francisco—have decided that their law enforcement officers will not take action against illegal immigrants they discover while performing their duties. For example, officers will not inquire about the legal status of a person who is apprehended for criminal activity. Even when they have an illegal immigrant in custody for committing a crime, they will not bother to determine that person's immigration status. Apparently, there are so many illegals in many of these cities that the powers that be have just decided to let that category of criminal behavior go unpunished.

A major problem with these sanctuary cities is that they are magnets for illegal immigrants. The word has long been out regarding which cities are most likely to cover these people's premeditated, illegal entry. So, their goal becomes getting into the country one way or another, and then heading to a sanctuary city where they will remain virtually undetected.

Another major problem is that the illegals have to cross through other areas to get to these sanctuaries, and residents and law enforcement personnel in other jurisdictions must bear the burden thanks to the lax law enforcement practiced in these so-called "safe havens." Thus, what's safe for an illegal immigrant in a sanctuary city creates dangerous circumstances not only for its own legal residents, but also for the legal residents of other cities, towns and rural areas.

While traveling in other countries, I never heard of such a "sanctuary" option for foreigners—most other countries would never put up with it. They think it is just as stupid as you and I do, and they laugh at us for tolerating such tripe.

On May 21, 2006, I sat in on an update briefing by the staff of Governor Rick Perry (R-TX). I must admit that the meeting was enlightening regarding many of the issues facing Texas today, but with one glaring exception: What is being done about the threats that the State of Texas faces because the federal government is not defending our borders?

The head of Homeland Security operations in Texas talked about many of the threats facing the country and put forth the standard party line. However, when asked a specific question about what we can do about sanctuary cities, he belittled the questioner, did not answer the inquiry, and went right back to his party line.

Was this event an example of government trying to keep the people quiet, or was it just a mistake on the part of an unseasoned staff member? More likely, it's a simple matter of having policies in place that tend to brief well, but when you dig a little deeper, there really isn't much substance.

I'm not saying that what many of our politicians are doing is not hard work. It's just that the work they are doing is, unfortunately, not very efficient. Based on the fact that we continue to be overrun with illegals, drug traffickers and the like, it's obvious that our current operations are not very effective. And there are two reasons for this: inefficient law enforcement policy and unscrupulous lawyers.

For example, in 1979, Los Angeles Police Chief Daryl Gates initiated Special Order 40, which prohibits officers from initiating police action where the objective is to discover the alien status of a person.[120] In other words, this order prevents police officers from checking immigration status of a suspect. It also prevents them from informing the appropriate federal officials of a person's immigration status.[121] As if that's not enough, Los Angeles no longer checks for proof of insurance during traffic stops because of "cries of racism and pending lawsuits from immigrant groups."[122]

Another issue I've read about is the desire, in many states, to deny social services to illegal immigrants. An example is Oklahoma's House Bill 1804, which denies illegal aliens state identification cards. It also requires state and local agencies to verify the citizenship status of applicants before authorizing benefits and gives state and local law enforcement officials the power to enforce federal immigration laws. In addition, it requires employers to enter job applicants into an electronic immigration database to verify legal status.[123] To me, this only makes sense—yet judges keep dictating that we are "required" by our Constitution to provide social services to people who are not even citizens of our country. I say, this is *our* country, and here, the *majority* makes the decisions. Still, time and again, the courts dictate that the states cannot deny certain services to illegal immigrants just because they are not U.S. citizens. Does that make any sense at all?

In Houston, Texas, the Harris County Hospital District is experiencing a huge increase in healthcare demand from illegal immigrants. In just a year, their costs have jumped seventy-seven percent over the previous three years, to almost $100 million. Hospital district spokesman Bryan McLeod stated, "The costs are increasing because the population of undocumented immigrants is increasing and the cost of health care is rising."[124] Notice his political correctness—using the phrase "undocumented immigrants" rather than calling them what they really are: illegal immigrants.

Will somebody please show me what part of our Constitution tells us to treat illegals as if they were U.S. citizens? No one can, obviously, because the requirement does not come from the Constitution, as we have already discovered. It comes from activist courts and politicians who apparently have some other agenda besides protecting their own constituents.

To make matters worse, time after time, the courts declare many state legislatures' attempts to deny social services to illegal immigrants either unconstitutional or treading on the jurisdiction of the federal government. Some examples are California's Proposition 187 initiative in 1994 and Texas' *Plyler v. Doe* case. Oklahoma's HB 1804 is an exception; it has withstood two court challenges.

Despite the challenges, the states persist—according to the National Conference of State Legislatures, some 500 immigration-reform bills were introduced in 2006.[125] But what recourse is there for state governments trying to rectify the situation in which they find themselves? This state of affairs is the direct result of our federal government's inaction. It is also the result of a court system that apparently cannot deliver opinions strictly based on the U.S. Constitution, but insists on usurping the role of lawmakers with socially biased decisions. In the face of that, what are state governments to do?

Well, for one, they can stop trying to pass legislation that makes it easier for illegal immigrants to exist in this country. Take, for example, the case of the *matricula consular* card, a form of identification that the Mexican government issues to its citizens, similar to a Social Security card, passport or driver's license. A person who possesses this card has proof that he or she is a citizen of Mexico. One major problem with this ID card is that it is relatively easy to forge. As you are probably aware, the fraudulent document industry blossomed along with the illegal immigration of millions into the United

States. These days, illegal immigrants are able to obtain just about any document they need for residence in the United States if they have the money to buy it.

And the problem with the relative ease of creating fake *matricula consular* cards? There are initiatives in some state governments to allow people to use them as a legitimate form of identification when seeking certain services such as banking, applying for a loan, or obtaining credit or a driver's license. Why would state governments push for this? The answer is rather simple: By allowing its use, they will be getting more people to do business with the banking industry, the state motor vehicle agency, insurance agencies and so on. They will be generating customers and facilitating business. It does not matter to some of the corrupt politicians who try to push such legislation through that such acts would give people who are here illegally the tools they need to gain a semblance of normalcy and even quasi-legal status in our country. These politicians just could not care less whether these people are here illegally or not.

As it stands, according to Congressman Gary Miller, more than 350 financial institutions accept the *matricula consular* card, so many illegal immigrants already have access to mainstream financial services. In addition, Congressman Miller cites the fact that a "regulation in the federal budget prohibited U.S. businesses from accepting these cards, but an amendment passed September 14, 2004, pulls this requirement."[126]

It appears that it all comes down to a matter of money. But whose money is it in the end? Actually, it's yours, in the form of taxes that go toward subsidizing this criminal activity. It's all a vicious cycle—but we surely can do something about it despite the politicians who just do not care about the average citizen who is just trying to make a better life for his children. We keep hearing that the illegals come here to find better lives; how about turning some attention to the legal citizens who are trying to do the same thing?

Chapter Twelve

Myths About Illegal Immigration

Let's say that you know a person whom you regard as your friend, and that person continually takes advantage of you. Despite your efforts at goodwill, the guy just will not turn his life around. Time and again, he deceives you; he borrows money and never pays you back. Moreover, the situation presents no indication that it will ever improve. Is this person actually your friend?

We should ask ourselves whether Mexico is really our friend. President Bush has stated repeatedly that it is, but I find myself questioning whether this is indeed the case. The threats coming to us from Mexico are arguably the most immediate threats to our national sovereignty and national security, even though they come subtly. Mexico deceives us, steals from us (remittances), allows the transport of illegal drugs through their country *en route* to ours, assists terrorists entering our land and facilitates the mass exodus of their citizenry so they can enter our country illegally.

Furthermore, as a nation it aids and abets drug gangs and syndicates that spread death throughout our nation and hold American people who live close to their trafficking corridors hostage. They have exhibited all this "friendliness" toward our nation for years—and they do not attempt to change.

We have tried to improve the lives of many Mexican citizens through foreign aid, medical help, infrastructure improvement, counter-drug operations, trade agreements such as NAFTA and CAFTA, and the list goes on.

NAFTA is mainly beneficial to Mexico, with some benefit to the United States and almost none to Canada. I would say that this is indicative of the fact that we are trying very hard to lift up Mexico—but apparently all of our efforts are not enough to turn its economy or its leadership around.

According to a congressional report, some members of Congress are beginning to question the benefits of NAFTA because what was a trade surplus with Mexico is now a trade deficit. Starting in 2004, we had a $45 billion trade deficit with Mexico—and that deficit is increasing annually.[127]

Ask yourself whether you would remain in a personal relationship that was as extremely one-sided as the one we find ourselves in with Mexico. I am willing to bet that you would not. So, why is the U.S. government continuing to allow Mexico to take advantage of us? Conceptually, I just do not get it.

Nor do I get the argument that illegal immigrants are only here "seeking work" and not escaping the sometimes dire situations of their home countries. It may very well be true that they're looking to make some money, but you have to look beyond the pretense of the statement and see things for what they really are. I even heard a Mexican official comment on talk radio that illegal immigrants do not go to America for work—they go to make more money because they cannot make enough to support their families in Mexico.

This highlights the fact that Mexico's unemployment rate was, until the recent economic downturn, an extremely low 3.6 percent.[128] However, the official's assertion that Mexican nationals are seeking higher wages is simply another poor excuse given by a spokesman for an irresponsible Mexican government. If they eliminated their institutionalized corruption, then they would have both the will and resources to fix their social and economic problems without having to rely on the United States.

If our government really wanted to remedy our current crisis, they would not deny the real problem—that the countries of origin of many of the illegals are to blame. That's right: We, as a nation, are not the problem—other nations are. And as long as our government allows them to abuse all U.S. citizens, the situation will never change for the better.

Another argument I do not understand is that illegal immigrants pay U.S. taxes. This statement is so much rubbish; it's the same old diatribe promulgated by the leftist apparatus in all of its many and varied forms. The only taxes we can safely assume all illegals pay are sales taxes. Consider that many illegal laborers are not on the books and that they receive their wages in cash, which means that their employers are not withholding any of the taxes that are required of the rest of us. I have talked to business owners who have used the tactics I just described, so I know that it's really happening.

"But we cannot do without them," some people say, citing the faulty argument that without illegal workers, our economy would crumble. This is another ludicrous statement. It may be true that American workers are reluctant to take certain jobs because the wages are not sufficient. But since illegal immigrants are willing to do the work at the lower wages, they *are* taking work away from Americans. Without the availability of illegal labor, wages would be higher, and Americans would be doing the work. So, why can't we get on with our lives without all the illegal immigrants who are in our country? As we say in Texas, "That dog just won't hunt."

Another factor we should bear in mind is that some sectors of our economy have seen the writing on the wall. For example, the agricultural industry is working toward alternative cultivation methods; remember, necessity generates innovation. The agricultural folks are realizing that, first, even illegal immigrant labor is getting more expensive, and second, America may get serious about illegal immigrants coming into this country. They are starting to find themselves with limited options, so many are turning to mechanization to answer the needs of their harvesting efforts. They have to do this or risk their competitiveness in the market place.

Actually, the overabundance of illegal immigrant labor that has been available for decades is one of the main reasons why there has not been more mechanization of certain agricultural harvests. However, just as there are machines that do almost every aspect of a road construction operation, there will soon be mechanical options for growers to use in their harvesting operations.

Still, so many people say that we cannot deport them all. To that, I say, "Oh, really?" Let me be straightforward: I believe that many Americans would be ecstatic if we just got around to deporting several million of the 35 million or so illegal immigrants who are here right now. Don't believe me? Let's do an honest poll and find out what the American public thinks. I am confident that many would say that we just need to get on with what must be done to protect our way of life—and the livelihoods of countless Americans—instead of bowing to the irrational leftists and internationalists.

In the 1920s and 1930s, we returned an estimated one to two million illegal immigrants to Mexico. At that time, we were enduring the Great Depression, so I can begin to understand why so many illegals entered our country in hopes of finding work *and* why we deported so many of them—because there were not enough jobs for our own citizens.

There was another mass deportation of illegal immigrants in the 1950s, when newly elected President Eisenhower took action against all of the illegal immigrants in the United States. At this time, the primary lawbreakers were from Mexico, so they became the focus of what came to be called "Operation Wetback." At this time, there were an estimated three million Mexican nationals in the United States illegally. The operation began in the north and worked its way southward with very good results. The Immigration and Naturalization Service (INS) returned thousands to Mexico—and thousands more who realized that America was serious fled back to Mexico of their own accord.

So, why are we consistently told that we can't deport them all? The reality is that we have already completed successful deportations in our past, and I do not know of any reason that we cannot accomplish another at this time. If we firmly enforce our border security this time, we would probably never need to deport *en masse* again.

Of course, we must ensure that those who are deported are treated with dignity and respect during their deportations. Let no one misunderstand me: We should treat all human beings in a manner that is becoming of a traditionally Judeo-Christian nation such as ours.

Successful historical deportations are evidence that deportations work to rid this country of illegal immigrants. Yet, some people still worry that such an undertaking might mean that some of the *wrong* people get deported as well—namely, U.S. legal residents and even citizens. This one is beyond me. I have every confidence that legal residents of this country would have appropriate identification to verify their status and would have no problem producing it should the need arise. I have no problem with law enforcement officers checking my identification to ensure that I am a U.S. citizen.

Nor do I have a problem with what is called "criminal profiling," even when it is being done to me, as long as it's in the name of keeping our country safe. I was criminally profiled by law enforcement a couple times. Once was when I was driving on a highway in Kansas. I was doing the speed limit, but I was a young, white male driving a new, red Corvette convertible with out-of-state plates. The trooper cruised up behind me and after a few minutes, he pulled out and around me.

When I got home, I went to visit a friend of mine who was a deputy sheriff and asked him why the trooper had done that to me. After all, I was a law-abiding citizen who was serving his country. My friend told me that I fit the profile for a drug dealer, and that that was why the state trooper had run a check on my plates.

A similar situation happened when I was stationed in the panhandle of Florida. This time I was driving on Highway 98, late at night, in a Chevy 3500 king cab, dually pickup truck. A police officer pulled up behind me and then drove off after a few minutes. Later, I went to a neighbor of mine who was a deputy sheriff, recalled the events to him and then asked him why he thought the police officer had done that. He said that I fit the profile for a drug dealer and that I was driving on a major Texas-Florida drug-trafficking route; therefore, the police officer had checked me out.

I guess this is where I'm supposed to scream about having my civil rights violated, right? My answer is, unequivocally, "no." Now why is that my answer? Because I know that we are in a drug war and that the police officers were doing their jobs, and I feel very good about that—and glad to have experienced the professionalism of those fine officers as they carried out their very important missions.

I also do not mind the fact that we are searched at airports these days, though some people feel it is a violation of their rights. What bothers *me*, really, is when a Middle Eastern male is not searched—even though all terrorist attacks against the U.S. to date have been made by Middle Eastern males between the ages of seventeen and thirty-five. Just how efficient is it of airport security to waste time with me, or say, an older woman?

This is evidence of what the leftists and progressives have brought on us through more of their political correctness. All the while, the government keeps attempting to keep us in line while the ship is sinking. It is as if they do not care about anything but keeping law-abiding citizens subdued. They do not realize that if the federal government would get some intestinal fortitude and do what needs to be done on the border, the majority of the American people would be behind them.

But let's get back to the matter of identification. How hard is it to keep on your person a copy of whatever documents are required to verify citizenship? While stationed in foreign countries, I knew that I had to have my military identification card with me at all times. When I travel abroad, I know that I should keep a copy of my passport with me at all times. So, cannot virtually all American citizens keep their driver's licenses or state-issued ID cards with them during this deportation timeframe? This is not rocket science. In my opinion, any Americans who are too lazy or irresponsible to comply with accepted procedure…well, perhaps they would wake up after some time in a detention facility.

But oh, wait, there aren't detention facilities for this purpose yet. While illegal immigrants continue to invade our country, how many times do we need to listen to representatives of our government tell us that we will begin to get our borders under control once we have the infrastructure we need in place, including bed space or detention space? How long does it take to throw up fencing, stock some bedding, assign a guard force and get on with the detention of all these criminals? We do not have to build Taj Mahals in which to incarcerate all of these illegal immigrants. Tents would do just fine; hopefully, once we begin to get serious about the illegals coming into our country, there will be fewer of them trying to enter, so we really will not need to waste time and money on elaborate facilities that will only be used temporarily.

As a soldier, I lived in the field for months on end, and I survived. These people who come in illegally know they are breaking our laws, and they know that they will have to make sacrifices for that decision. Do you really think that these people are accustomed to living in the lavish accommodations we intend to construct to detain them? Do they deserve better than our own servicemen and women?

As I have said, we must ensure that we treat all of these people with dignity and respect, but that is about as far as it goes. Place them in secure areas and let them sleep in tents. Of course, we would feed them a sufficient diet until we deport them. But can we ever get over the political correctness and stupid decisions made by some of the people who are in charge of certain aspects of policy implementation?

Sometimes, it seems like the answer to that is "no." Part of the problem is that so many people call upon our history as a "nation of immigrants." But the histories of virtually any country you could name include immigration of various sorts—including Mexico. This is just the same old, worn-out rhetoric; there is little to no comparison between the people of ages gone by, who came here to breathe freely, and the many unskilled and illiterate people who stream across our borders because they know that they can get away with it.

And in the midst of that, where are the discussions about accepting responsibility for your actions? It seems to be missing from the debate concerning appropriate disposition of those who broke our laws to enter this country—and then potentially continued to break a plethora of laws during the course of their stay here, including but not limited to a routine failure to pay taxes.

Now, I know that if I were to break the law, I would have to account for whatever I did. I've often wondered what I would do if I committed something particularly egregious and had to stand trial. I tell myself that I would forego any trial, admit my breach against society and take the punishment I was due. Maybe I am in the minority on that view of accountability, but I believe there are many Americans who still value honor and integrity, who might take the same tack as I on this point. I would like to think so, anyway.

We keep hearing all the reasons why we should not be so hard on those who blatantly break our laws. I wonder why? Is there something wrong with punishment for crime and deterrent against future crime? Or are there really any good arguments *for* illegal immigration? I have yet to hear or read any substantive or rational arguments in favor of it. I do hear many emotional reasons and false claims why the United States should allow all of the illegal immigrants into this country. Some examples:

"Americans are racists!" No, I do not believe this "reason" not to defend our borders for an instant, because this is a typical ploy of the leftists—and those who are guilty of something. I really like how this argument for illegals being in our country relies on so many facts and analyses that bear on the issue.

"America is xenophobic!" To be xenophobic means that you are afraid of foreigners and I do not think this is the reality in our country. I have been in many countries around the world, and I can honestly state that I was never afraid of any of the people simply because they were foreign to me. Now, I am not saying that I was not afraid for my life on numerous occasions. In many of these countries, people would murder foreigners for a few pennies—and I mean that literally. It's difficult to believe the reality of the quality of life and the state of affairs in some nations of the world.

"If the Americans build a barrier, they will make people feel bad." Then what are we supposed to do? Roll over and play dead, and let all of these people come into our country unabated because we do not want to hurt their feelings or make them think that they are *less* than anyone else? I'm getting tired of this line of irrational reasoning, in all of its forms, that seems to be permeating our mainstream media today.

"A fence would only trap illegal immigrants in the United States." Or, "I thought we were working toward a world without barriers." These are typical leftist sound bites to see what will resonate with the public. Of course, there is no rational foundation for such statements. A fence would accomplish several objectives as long as we strengthen our interdiction and internal law enforcement efforts to combat illegal immigration.

A quick counter-argument to these anti-fence arguments is that, as experience shows, good fences make good neighbors. Think about it: I have some great neighbors, and that is in part because we all have fences. One of my neighbors in particular has a big dog and I think that our friendship would be sorely strained if neither of us had a fence and that dog could go freely into and out of my own property, using my lawn as he pleased.

Do the fences at Fort Knox keep people more honest than they would be if there were no barriers around the gold and precious treasures in the facility? I think the answer is, absolutely, "Yes." How about our military bases? Our prison facilities? The White House? I think it is a no-brainer that fences deter inappropriate behavior.

So what are we doing here? How many sacrifices are required of the American people in order to lift up Mexico? Would it not be more prudent to straighten out our economy here in America and simultaneously get serious about bringing about meaningful change in Mexico? We can continue to keep the American people in the dark, or we can start letting them know what the situation is and move forward from there.

But will that really happen? Signs point to no. This is politics as usual—a few pieces of enabling legislation here and there, each of which seems benign enough on its own, if we don't look more deeply at them. And if we don't, before we realize it, we are confronted with a mosaic that is definitely not what the voters want, and it's too late to change it.

Chapter Thirteen

Economics

The economic effects on the "losing" countries in this immigration war—that would include the United States—are far-reaching. Though you may not realize it, the high prices you pay for many goods and services are caused by the presence of illegal immigrants and drug-related crime in our country. Moreover, your taxes would be much lower if those who do not legally belong here were not draining our social services systems.

For all that they take from our country in the form of public assistance, healthcare and education, illegal immigrants do not in turn stimulate our economy by spending the money they earn from us here. More often, their wages go toward remittances—the money that they send back to their home countries, totaling in the billions every year. Many Latin American countries have become reliant on this economic relationship, which drains U.S. resources. Many governments even encourage their citizens to migrate to America just for this reason.

In a word, remittances are big business and not just south of our border. The American financial industry, in all of its forms, lends a hand in the process—and earns a significant profit from it through fees for wire transfers, ATM transactions and sending money orders. Our own banking industry has a huge financial stake in the booming, illegal immigrant remittances industry.

One player in this game, I came to learn through some research, is the

Inter-American Development Bank (IDB). What is it? Where does it get its funding? What is it developing? As it turns out, it's a regional bank that "is the main source of multilateral financing and expertise for sustainable economic, social and institutional development in Latin America and the Caribbean."[129] Its mission is to bring a "better life... within the reach of millions of citizens in Latin America and the Caribbean—better housing, better health care and zero tolerance for corruption or discrimination."[130]

When I read this, I assumed that the IDB was yet another international lending organization receiving funding from the United States, but that was only partially accurate. The IDB receives money *indirectly* from the U.S. through the remittances that originate in this country and end up in the Latin American region. The IDB tracks remittances because they are "critical to the survival of millions of individual families, and the health of many national economies throughout Latin America and the Caribbean (LAC)."[131] Remittances also facilitate the spread of "financial democracy,"[132] whatever that means.

In other words, this non-governmental organization looks upon remittances as a way to redistribute economic stimulus from one country, namely the United States, to the third world and undeveloped countries within the Western Hemisphere. In 2005, the IDB reported that remittances to Latin American countries totaled an estimated $55 billion.[133] The top beneficiaries, in billions of dollars, were[134]:

1. Mexico: $20
2. Brazil: $6.4
3. Colombia: $4.1
4. Guatemala: $3
5. El Salvador: $2.8
6. Peru: $2.5
7. Dominican Republic: $2.4
8. Ecuador: $2.0
9. Honduras: $1.7
10. Jamaica: $1.7
11. Haiti: $1.1.

By 2007, the above numbers grew, in billions of dollars, to[135]:

1. Mexico: $23.9
2. Brazil: $7.1
3. Colombia: $4.5
4. Guatemala: $4.1
5. El Salvador: $3.7
6. Peru: $3.9
7. Dominican Republic: $3.1
8. Ecuador: $3.1
9. Honduras: $2.6
10. Jamaica: $1.9
11. Haiti: $1.8.

From 2005 to 2007, the total for remittances to the LAC, based on the top eleven recipients, increased from $45.8 billion to $59.7 billion.[136] Mexico alone neared $24 billion *per annum*—a large part of their economy considering that in 2005 their oil exports accounted for $28 billion of their economic output.[137] Imagine Mexico adding that much into its economy every year without really doing anything to get it, and you can see why remittances are quite a windfall for them and for many Latin American nations.

But this good fortune for them comes at the expense of our country. There is no incentive for Mexico to stop its citizenry from illegally entering the United States. Remember that illicit drug trafficking generates an estimated $65 billion a year for Mexico; the remittances from its citizens within our country—many of them here illegally—are its second- or third-largest source of revenue depending on the price of oil. So, why should they change?

On top of this, our government is considering offering, in essence, illegal Mexican immigrants further financial assistance by entering into a Social Security totalization agreement with Mexico. According to the Social Security Administration (SSA), totalization agreements provide for[138]:

1. Elimination of dual Social Security taxation that occurs when a worker from one country works in another country and is

required to pay Social Security taxes to both countries on the same earnings.

2. Allows workers to combine work credits from both countries to become eligible for benefits. The benefit amount paid is proportional to the amount of credits earned in the paying country.

The United States has existing agreements with Australia (2002), Canada (1984), Chile (2001), Greece (1994), Ireland (1993), Italy (1978), Republic of Korea (2001), United Kingdom (1985) and many Western European countries (generally enacted between 1979 and 1993). The SSA has concluded that a totalization agreement with Mexico would not be detrimental to our Social Security system and that any adverse effects would be negligible at best.

I, however, contend that there are some fundamental disadvantages that would result should we go forward with such an agreement with Mexico.

To illustrate why, let's look at the difference between our agreement with Canada and the one proposed for Mexico. The fundamental dynamic in play is quite different between a Canadian who comes to work in America and someone who comes from Mexico. The Canadian worker is coming to work temporarily. The Mexican worker, because of his country's less-than-attractive economic environment, may be coming with the intention to work here long-term. To compound the situation, Congress has been debating whether or not to give constructive credit to illegal immigrants for the time they've worked in America illegally. The danger is that this leads to credit in our Social Security system and creates an incentive for illegal immigrants to continue to come to America.

In addition, the Mexican system requires twenty-four years of work to earn vestment, in contrast to the U.S.' ten-year requirement, and the benefits we offer are much greater. These are yet more incentives for people to come to America with no intention of ever leaving.

One way to make such an idea less appealing would be to overhaul the Social Security totalization agreements—or even to get rid of them and have temporary workers pay into the systems from their countries of origin instead. If we knew that certain workers were only in this country temporarily, could we not just remove any requirement to pay into U.S. Social Security, thus removing the potential to earn credits in the system along with any incentive for them to stay?

With today's technology, it should be an easy matter to develop the appropriate automated systems to track these workers and transmit their Social Security taxes back to their parent countries. Why should we be collecting for Social Security benefits that these people will never draw in our country?

Chapter Fourteen

Jobs Americans Will Do

I wonder why certain people in the business community support a guest worker program. I also wonder why the unions have been rather silent on this entire issue. It appears that certain sectors of our economy stand to make more profit by using cheap, illegal immigrant labor rather than by using American labor. Let us not be naïve about it, as there is big money at stake here.

The first reason is that many businesses are only interested in their bottom lines and their ability to make money. To me it is very sad to think that some would sell us out rather than do what they must know to be right and just.

Who are some obvious perpetrators? Maybe businesses in the construction, restaurant and hospitality, agricultural, medical, banking, professional (including education and legal) and services (including financial) industries. The media routinely targets the construction, restaurant, hospitality and agriculture industries as requiring illegal immigrant labor since Americans just will not do the jobs that these businesses need done.

Another reason that comes to mind is that some politicians believe they can gain the support of these illegals and bring them into the electorate as their supporters. I believe that President George W. Bush has aggressively courted the Hispanic vote for many years—and we know that many leftists have. There is nothing wrong with this *per se*, but they should be trying to gain the support of legal Hispanic voters—not the illegal ones. When I was campaigning, I found it interesting that the Republicans of Hispanic origin drastically favored doing something to rectify our illegal immigrant crisis.

The problem is that the big bucks are going into the pockets of the big businesses, and much of the wages earned by illegals returns to their countries of origin as remittances, as we discussed before. That money is being siphoned right out of our economy—with no return. And all this happens at the expense of the honest, tax-paying American citizen.

As it stands now, we, the tax-paying public, are subsidizing the industries that make money exploiting the use of illegal labor. As we continue to subsidize these businesses, they pay these workers what amounts to slave wages. Where is the liberal outrage? These poor people are no more than slaves to some business owners.

In addition, since many of these businesses do not keep track of payroll, they do not pay taxes of any kind for the work these laborers perform. These employers pay their laborers in cash under the table—with no workman's comp, no 401(k)s, and no bookkeeping for health insurance, federal taxes and Social Security. I think you have the picture by now.

When I retired from the U.S. Army and moved back to my homeland of Texas, I had some work done on my new home. I had a new cooling and heating system installed, I bought some furniture and had it delivered, and I had some plumbing and electrical work done.

After being gone for thirty years, I remembered that it is important to have a reliable air conditioner when you are living in Texas. As the worker installed my outside unit, I made my usual inquiry: "How's business?" He replied, "I used to get $600 a day for an installation job like this, and now I only get $200 for the same amount of work."

I thought that was a drastic change, so I asked, "Why is that?" He then explained that some of their competitors were using illegal immigrant labor. So, in order to stay in business, they had to pay their workers lower wages.

When the plumbers, electricians and movers came out to my house, I asked the same questions. I got close to the same story from each of them. The responses were slightly different, but they all boiled down to the same thing: Their businesses were suffering because some of their competitors were using illegal labor.

The short version is that illegal immigrant labor drives down wages, puts many small businesses out of business, and leaves otherwise qualified Americans unemployed. Some estimates put the cost of lost-depressed wages at $200 billion a year because of immigrants (legal and illegal) working for lower wages and taking Americans' jobs.[139]

Another example stems from the aftermath of Hurricane Katrina and the clean-up efforts that ensued. There was a call for laborers to come to the disaster area and assist in the clean up. An employment service from Mobile, Alabama, received a request for 270 workers and responded by sending, initially, about seventy. However, after a couple of weeks, the men were fired because the Mexicans had arrived—the employers let the Americans go because the Hispanic and Latino workers would work for less.[140] A story in a Mexican magazine went on to say that conservative estimates put the total number of Hispanic and Latino workers who invaded the Gulf Coast states after Hurricane Katrina at 30,000.[141]

Now, if we decided to return all or even most of the illegal immigrants to their own countries, the effects on our economy would not be like turning off a light switch. Just the process of identifying and processing all of the illegal immigrants for deportation would take quite some time to accomplish. But still, there is a way to do it.

Of course, as the first step we would have to seal our borders to prevent any further illegal entry (or most of it, anyway). Then, the gradual diminishing of the illegal population would begin through voluntary deportation and law enforcement action. It would not be as if Americans would wake up one morning and realize that there were no longer any illegal immigrants in our country. It would be a gradual process.

Since the removal of the illegal immigrants would take quite some time to accomplish, the increase in the costs of various industries would also be similarly gradual. For example, as companies employed citizens instead of cheap, slave labor to, for example, build houses, the cost of buying a home might gradually start to rise. If it took a fifty-percent increase in wages to motivate Americans to take jobs building houses, then we would start to realize a corresponding increase in the cost of buying a new home. This is just how it would have to be. Now, we can either accept this fact or keep subsidizing the industries that routinely use illegal immigrant labor to enhance their profits with our hard-earned tax dollars.

However, it is also probable that the higher wages being paid to American workers would help stimulate our economy in other ways—primarily through consumer spending and lower unemployment. Add to this the reduced social systems costs and potentially lower taxes that would result, as well as a potential decrease in utilities due to reduced demand. Thus, you can see how the economic effects of deportation are likely to be far less than the leftists, internationalists and some business lobbies would like you to believe.

The U.S. economy is strong and resilient. Hurricanes Katrina and Rita gave some evidence to the fact that America can withstand enormous disruption and still forge ahead. Let us not forget the massive effect of the terrorist attacks on our economy after the events of September 11, 2001. Yes, it was a tough row to hoe for America for quite some time, but we pulled together and made it through that horrific time in our national history. And for this situation, we can do it again.

It's likely that with the positive effects of deportation on our economy and infrastructure, negative effects would soon be offset. Therefore, if the U.S. economy could withstand September 11, it can easily withstand the conversion of our U.S. labor force to include citizens and legal immigrants only—without a so-called guest worker program.

Chapter Fifteen

Removing the Incentives

Once—and if—our border is secure, it will still be necessary to remove the incentives that attract illegal immigrants to our country if we are to rectify the problem. Even though the border will be closed, we will still need to make entry very unattractive. This will encourage illegal immigrants who are already here to deport themselves, which will reduce the scale and cost to taxpayers of our own deportation effort.

One thing we can do toward this end is establish an English-language-speaking requirement for all who live here. I remember when I was stationed at Nellis Air Force Base near Las Vegas, Nevada. At the time, I was training reining horses, but that's another story, though I bring it up because of a conversation I had with a man who delivered some hay to me on one occasion. As we tried to talk, as I often do with workers, I realized that this man did not speak very much English. Up to that time, I had paid little attention to the illegal immigrant problem, and this was in 1999, so it did not occur to me that the man might be here illegally.

He said that he had recently moved from California to Nevada. Then he said he figured that he was going to have to learn English because there were not many people around Las Vegas who spoke Spanish. There was no fear or apprehension in his voice. He was just very matter of fact on the subject. That leads me to believe that there are other like-minded people who come to our country and are more than willing to learn English. However, the current situation is such that many immigrants do not feel any urgency to learn our language because they do not have to do so.

Have you ever traveled in Eastern Europe? I can tell you that as far as foreign languages go, not only is Russian difficult to speak, but it is also difficult to learn Cyril. In addition, there are no signs in English there. If you make a telephone call to a government agency, there are no options to receive information in another language. So what must a person do? Learn the language.

The liberals like to say that it is not good for a person's well-being, to feel that he is not liked because he is in a place where nobody speaks his language. You know, this never crossed my mind in all of my travels in foreign countries. I never thought of myself as a lesser person because I could not speak Russian or German upon first arrival in these countries. And, in fact, I learned quite a bit of German while I was stationed there. The leftist misinformation on this issue is just more nonsense to get people off of the real issue which is that we as Americans, at least where I live, want English as the official language in this country. The polling data bears this out as well.

While this requirement is put in place, some others should be removed—namely, the requirement that teachers be bilingual—unless, of course, they teach foreign languages. The practice of hiring only bilingual teachers, which happens especially in the southwest, is ridiculous. I know that in theory this sounds good, but such a policy discriminates against our own fully qualified teachers who only speak English. What districts are left with, often, is a teacher who speaks some form of Spanish but is not too proficient in the subject matter he is hired to teach.

It has become obvious that over time, our education, health care, welfare, social security and legal systems have become major incentives for foreigners to come to this country. A significant reason why a life in the United States is so coveted is that the realities associated with living in many other countries are quite harsh by comparison. Having lived in and visited many countries around the world, I have to say that there is absolutely no place like the United States; no place has what we have. A few countries come close, but they are nothing like our great country.

Where else can a person go *illegally* and receive education benefits as if they were citizens? I know of no place that allows illegal immigrants to attend its schools as we do in the United States.

Remember what we learned earlier: Texas alone spends about $6 billion per year educating non-English-speaking children. If we remove this incentive, we will not only deter further illegal immigration—we will save a lot of money as well.

Take away also their Social Security, free medical care (except for life-threatening emergencies), food stamps, WIC, low-income housing and so on and the United States starts to look less and less attractive to illegal immigrants.

Chapter Sixteen

Amnesty Versus Assimilation

Is it prudent to legalize millions of people who have absolutely no love for this great country of ours? Some of them are here for all of the right reasons, I'm sure, but a significant number of them are not. Would we be doing what is right for America by giving these people citizenship and the corresponding right to vote?

At one of the pro-immigrant rallies I saw on television, I heard people chanting, "Today we march, and tomorrow we vote!" What was that, some sort of threat? Are we supposed to just lie down and concede all of the hard-won accomplishments of our forebears? The leftist and internationalist elitists think that we should.

Well, I do not, and I will not.

This whole idea is rather disconcerting to me. I see people on TV chanting, "*Reconquista!*" and "*revolucion*!" Is that supposed to make me comfortable with a mass amnesty or a massive guest worker program that means citizenship in the end? I do not believe this is what the majority of Americans want.

If the federal government grants amnesty to all of the immigrants in California, it would be shifting the responsibility for funding for programs such as education, incarceration, law enforcement, health care and welfare from itself to the state governments. This is because once an illegal immigrant becomes a legal citizen, he is no longer the responsibility of the federal government. Thus, rather than spending the resources necessary to keep the illegal immigrants out and remove the ones already here, the federal government simply makes them U.S. citizens through amnesty, and they become responsibilities of the individual states.

According to a California Health Institute study, it takes at least two generations for immigrants to become economically successful,[142] which means that they could be a burden on the system for quite a while. Keep in mind also that illegal immigrants do not contribute as much into the social services revenue stream as they consume, even if they often benefit only indirectly. For example, illegal immigrant parents of an alien born in the U.S. do not qualify for food stamps, but their child does. In addition, there's Aid to Families with Dependent Children (AFDC), a federal benefit package—and a form of welfare—that is available to illegal immigrant parents of an alien born in the U.S. The AFDC's eligibility requirements hinge on the status of the child and not on the status of either parent. All totaled, these and other welfare benefits and social services are costing the American taxpayers an estimated $90 billion a year.[143]

But to get back to the issue of legalization, we must think these issues through to their natural conclusions. If we suddenly make millions of illegal immigrants citizens of the United States, we also suddenly give the right to vote to millions of people who may have no regard for our nation's laws or self-governing existence. This is a frightening prospect, and another deliberate affront to our national sovereignty. When such an approach is used for purposes other than those in the best interests of preserving the Union, it is an attempt to affect change through the misuse of our democratic process of elections. To allow suddenly so many people the right to vote is a move toward the disenfranchisement of our legal citizens.

Given all that we have to put up with, I really get tired of being told that the majority of Americans aren't informed, that they really don't comprehend the issues or that what they say they want is over the top. And the real clincher is that many of our own representatives—at both state and federal levels—tell us they have to do "that which is for our own good, and not necessarily that which we want." That quote is from a conversation I had with my congressman some twenty years ago.

Again, this is, absolutely, not the way the Founders envisioned our representative form of government. In "The Federalist No. 45" and "The Federalist No. 46," James Madison discussed why there was no justification in fearing a centralization of power in the federal government:

> The powers delegated by the proposed Constitution to the federal government, are few and defined. Those which are to remain in the State Governments are numerous and indefinite. The former would be exercised principally on external objects, as war, negotiation, foreign commerce... The powers reserved to the several States would extend to all the objects, which, in the ordinary course of affairs, concern the lives, liberties, and properties of the people; and the internal order, improvement, and prosperity of the State...[144]
>
> The Federal and State Governments are in fact but different agents and trustees of the people, instituted with different powers for different purposes...[145] [T]he first and most natural attachment of the people would be to the governments of their respective States...[146] By the superintending care of these, all the more domestic and personal interests of the people would be regulated and provided for. With the affairs of these, the people would be more familiarly and minutely conversant...[147] It has been already proved, that the members of the federal would be more dependent on the members of the State governments, than the latter would be on the former...[148] A local spirit would infallibly prevail much more in the members of the Congress, than a national spirit would prevail in the Legislatures of the particular States.[149]

Now, I ask you to read Madison's words once again and then ask yourself if his vision is the reality we are witnessing in our government these days.

Representatives are supposed to vote in accordance with the desires of their constituents. Originally, the state legislatures were the ones with the power because the enumerated powers of the federal government were few, and every other power remained with the state governments. The states were sovereign, and their state officials were closest to the people; therefore, they would be more knowledgeable of the true desires of their voters. It was understood that the legislatures of the different states were primarily concerned with the specific interests of their home states.

At the federal level, it was also understood that the legislators were, first and foremost, to represent their constituencies back home. These precepts have been diluted to such a severe degree that some people now believe it is the duty of federal representatives to subordinate the interests of their own constituencies to the "greater" and "more important" considerations at the national level.

Why is there such a marked difference between what the polls are telling us and what our elected politicians are doing—or better yet, not doing—regarding the illegal immigrants in our country? Some polling data from Gallup (March 27, 2006) showed that eighty percent of Americans want the government to do something about illegal immigrants our country. A Quinnipiac University Poll (March 3, 2006) revealed that sixty-two percent of Americans do not want to make it easier for illegal immigrants to become citizens.[150]

In 2006, Senator Specter (R-PA) introduced Senate Bill 2611 (S.2611), the Comprehensive Immigration Reform Act of 2006. The bill's six cosponsors were Senators Brownback (R-KS), Graham (R-SC), Hagel (R-NE), Kennedy (D-MA), Martinez (R-FL) and McCain (R-AZ). The Senate passed the bill by a vote of 62–36. However, the House of Representatives rejected S.2611.

It is worthwhile to look at this bill because it is indicative of a legislative body that may have some members whose agendas are not in keeping with the desires of their constituencies. It also serves to shed some light on the various aspects in play in the comprehensive immigration reform debate.

An interesting note: The Republican senators voted 32–23 against the bill's passage and that the Democrats voted 38–4 in favor. Wait a minute… I thought this was Republican legislation. S.2611's problem was that it was in direct conflict with fundamental, Republican principles, and it was therefore not Republican—regardless of the fact that Republicans sponsored it.

This is a prime example of what irritates true Republicans and may even cause them to vote for a non-Republican candidate. After all, Republican candidates who push this kind of lunacy are not Republican, are they?

While reading S.2611, I began to think that perhaps there was no actual amnesty for illegal immigrants contained therein after all. However, I kept reading, and in the last thirty pages of one of its sections, there it was. It did not specify that exact term, but there was certainly evidence of amnesty within the bill.

The title of the section where I found the idea was "SEC. 601. Access to Earned Adjustment and Mandatory Departure and Reentry." The section began with some requirements that had to be met in order for an alien to "earn" an adjustment to his immigration status. To begin with, the alien had to provide evidence that he had been in the United States for five years before April 5, 2006 and had worked for an aggregate of three years within that five-year period; various exceptions to the preceding law were cited. Then, the act explained what documents an alien had to provide in order to show evidence of employment:

> (iv) EVIDENCE OF EMPLOYMENT
>
> (I) CONCLUSIVE DOCUMENTS-For purposes of satisfying the requirements in clause (i), the alien shall submit at least 2 of the following documents for each period of employment, which shall be considered conclusive evidence of such employment:
>
> (aa) Records maintained by the Social Security Administration.
>
> (bb) Records maintained by an employer, such as pay stubs, time sheets, or employment work verification.
>
> (cc) Records maintained by the Internal Revenue Service.
>
> (dd) Records maintained by a union or day labor center.
>
> (ee) Records maintained by any other government agency, such as worker compensation records, disability records, or business licensing records.[151]

Then came the real hammer to ensure enforcement. Pay special attention to subparagraph cc:

> (II) OTHER DOCUMENTS-An alien who is unable to submit a document described in subclause (I) may satisfy the requirement in clause (i) by submitting to the Secretary at least 2 other types of reliable documents that provide evidence of employment for each required period of employment, including:

(aa) bank records;
(bb) business records;
(cc) sworn affidavits from non-relatives who have direct knowledge of the alien's work, including the name, address, and phone number of the affiant, the nature and duration of the relationship between the affiant and the alien, and other verification information; or
(dd) remittance records.[152]

With all of the real requirements laid down in the proposed law, why did the Senate deem it appropriate to add what amounted to a silver-bullet escape clause? These people have been breaking our laws. Are we now expecting them to be forthright and honest with us and get sworn affidavits from their honest friends, telling our authorities that they really did work in the United States?

The ultimate escape from any of these requirements is the discretion of the Secretary of Homeland Security, who can waive any provision "for humanitarian purposes, to ensure family unity, or when it is otherwise in the public interest."[153] When taken altogether, is this not amnesty?

My next question is, "Who cares whether they've been working in our country or not?" Did they not break the law to get here? What difference does it make whether they were here for more than five years, less than five years, less than two years and so on? They broke the law to get here and continued to break laws each day that they decided to remain in America. No matter the category in which an illegal immigrant may fall, the path to citizenship may vary, but the result is nonetheless the same: citizenship.

The Senate bill also required current illegal immigrants to adjust their statuses *en route* to obtaining lawful permanent residence (LPR). All that a current illegal immigrant would have to do would be apply, wait a few years, and then earn LPR status (also called a "green card"); eventually he or she would become a U.S. citizen.[154] Even under the Deferred Mandatory Departure (DMD) plan, the illegal immigrants would possibly never have to leave the country. Nonetheless, they would remain on the coveted path to citizenship,[155] which could easily mean upwards of thirty-five million new, legal citizens in America in a matter of a few short years—as well as their millions of family members who could possibly come into the United States because of chain migration within the following few years.

The president's assertions that this is not amnesty ring hollow. Likewise, the affirmations of the Senate offer no comfort once we examine the facts of its bill. These elites attempt to pacify us while they force-feed another amnesty program on the American public.

In contrast to S.2611, the Senate subsequently passed S.6061, the Secure Fence Act of 2006, on September 29, 2006. The Secure Fence Act "[d]irects the Secretary of Homeland Security, within 18 months of enactment of this Act, to take appropriate actions to achieve operational control over U.S. international land and maritime borders."[156] The act further defines "operational control" as "...the prevention of all unlawful U.S. entries, including entries by terrorists, other unlawful immigrants, instruments of terrorism, narcotics, and other contraband."[157]

Lastly, the act "direct[s] the Secretary to provide at least two layers of reinforced fencing, installation of additional physical barriers, roads, lighting, cameras, and sensors extending" for approximately 700 miles along the U.S.-Mexico border by December 31, 2008.[158]

This legislation, S.6061, appears to be a step in the proper direction, but is it really all that it portends to be? Perhaps not. Here is the rub: S.6061 passed the Senate after S.5441, Department of Homeland Security Appropriations Act, 2007, which was in the fiscal year 2007 budget for the DHS. S.5441 included $1,187,565,000 in appropriations to DHS for border security fencing, infrastructure and technology. However, these monies were not sufficient to fund the 700 miles of fencing prescribed in S.6061. In other words, the Senate established the budget for the Department of Homeland Security, and then subsequently assigned a task that they had not funded monies to accomplish.

Was this oversight intentional? I wonder how many of the senators realized that there was no money previously appropriated in S.5441 for the 700 miles of fence when they voted for it in S.6061. The Senate's final vote on passage of this bill was 80–19 (record vote number: 262).[159]

I also wonder why so many naysayers suddenly jumped onboard to support this legislation by voting yea, including senators Boxer (D-CA), Clinton (D-NY), Feinstein (D-CA), McCain (R-AZ), Obama (D-IL), Schumer (D-

NY); Kennedy, who was present, was the only Senate member who did not vote on the bill?[160] Could it be that the members of the Senate knew that there were elections coming up in November 2006 and that the legislation did not guarantee a fence because there was no funding for it in S.5441? It would appear that many of the senators—primarily the Republican senators with help from their Democrat buddies—calculated all these events as a possible means to save face with their more conservative voters while not really doing anything substantive since there was no funding for the fence proposed in S.6061.

Let us take a moment to consider the comments that Senator Cornyn (R-TX) made regarding S.6061—and then you decide what motives might have led so many who have historically been against enforcement at the border to suddenly change their positions and their reasons for voting for the bill. Cornyn was quoted as stating: "It's one thing to authorize. It's another thing to actually appropriate the money and do it."[161] Remember that the appropriations bill, S.5441 had neither provisions nor funding for a 700-mile fence.

He also said, "Seven hundred miles of fencing would not solve the problem of illegal immigration because it would still leave about 1,300 miles of unfenced border. I am not sure that is the most practical use of that money."[162] This ranks up there with the typical leftist excuses. I would gladly take 700 miles of fence now and work for the remainder required later.

In addition, Senator Cornyn stated, "Voting for the fence was an important symbolic gesture to show that Congress is serious about protecting the border."[163] Now, tell me how anyone can construe a "symbolic gesture," in any way, shape, or form, to mean that you are serious about anything?

Two meaningful pieces of legislation put forth by the House of Representatives that the Senate should have subsequently passed but did not were H.R.6094 (Community Protection Act of 2006) and H.R.6095 (Immigration Law Enforcement Act of 2006). Each of these House resolutions passed with wide margins—328–95 and 277–140, respectively. The acts were not complicated. H.R.6094 "affirm[ed] that state and local law enforcement personnel have the inherent authority to investigate, identify, arrest, detain, or transfer to federal custody aliens in the United States"[164] and H.R.6095 provided for the detention and deportation of dangerous and criminal aliens, such as street gang members.[165]

Both of these were extremely important pieces of legislation that would have significantly contributed to the safety of American citizens. So why did the Senate not pass these bills? I know that I keep asking this, but where is the leadership in the Senate? The House of Representatives was at least trying to do its job. Why was the Senate not fulfilling its obligations?

When you really look at what's going on, it seems that many in the Senate are attempting to shield themselves, on one hand, from political fallout regarding their border security failures, while promoting the president's pro-amnesty agenda on the other hand.

PART IV
A FEDERAL SOLUTION

Chapter Seventeen

Instruments of National Power

In the realm of international relations or international politics, nations endeavor to perpetuate their respective national interests by attempting to influence other nations so as to benefit themselves. As we explore potential solutions for the southwest border of the United States, it is useful to understand those national capabilities from which we can draw to remedy that situation.

In general, nations derive their national power from such attributes as geography, natural resources, economy, culture, religion, customs, value system, language, citizenry, military strength and leadership. These national assets translate into the instruments of national power, which are diplomatic, economic, informational and military.

We must also understand that the traditional relationships are changing in that we are beginning to witness the emergence of influential non-state entities on the international scene. Transnational illicit drug cartels and terrorist organizations such as Hamas, Hezbollah and al-Qaeda are examples of such non-state entities. Therefore, we would be well-advised to temper the employment of our instruments of national power accordingly.

My point is that we cannot always deal with what are traditionally considered criminal activities—illicit drug trafficking or a terrorist blowing up a building—with a law enforcement mindset.

Let us discuss each instrument of national power in turn. The first is diplomacy, which typically manifests itself in the form of negotiations between nations in order to arrive at mutually acceptable agreements, alliances and treaties. However, for nations to arrive at reasonable and beneficial outcomes, the nations must be truly willing to talk.

Often, the diplomatic instrument alone is ineffective because the opposition does not really have anything to fear; diplomacy, after all, is mostly words. Remember Great Britain's prime minister, Neville Chamberlain, during the rise of Hitler? He uttered his famous words—"peace for our time"[166]—as he stood there holding up a piece of paper representing what he had negotiated with Hitler. However, as the diplomats were patting each other the back because they were successful in avoiding conflict, the Nazis cranked the engines of their panzers and started invading their neighbors. World War II was the result of the West's appeasement. You cannot appease tyrants.

These days, we have Iran, a tyrannical theocracy based on a flawed religion, and North Korea with its stereotypical, tyrannical, Communist dictator. Do you believe that we can reason with these countries? The answer is "no." Each of these nations is belligerent because each believes that it can get away with what it's doing. The ploys they use to extract benefits from the West include the development of nuclear weapons and their associated delivery systems.

Since I was stationed in the Republic of Korea twice, let me address some realities of what I think they are doing. First, every year I was there, the Communist north rattled its sabers about some issue or other with the intent of extracting badly needed resources from the West. North Korea is a failure, and it relies on this tactic each year to get what it wants.

Second, Kim Jong-Il knows what his fate would be—massive and debilitating retaliation, at least from the United States—should he be stupid enough to actually attack South Korea or any other country. Yet, he has no sincere intent to stop his nuclear program even when we give him that which he desires. If he actually were to do so, then he would lose his primary bargaining chip.

We can look at Iran in much the same manner. Iran is a defiant nation that exports terrorists around the globe and knows that nobody will do anything about it. In addition, it is pursuing a nuclear program that could result in the development of nuclear weapons.

When the rational nations of the world invaded Afghanistan and Iraq to destroy the terrorists, Iran appeared to be somewhat conciliatory. However, now that the U.S. is considering surrender, Iran is emboldened to continue its evil endeavors without any intent to stop. They have also stated that they will attack Israel if any nation tries to use force against them. In each of these cases, do you think that diplomacy is the answer? On the contrary, it appears that using the diplomatic instrument in isolation is not always effective.

The second instrument of national power is economics. This instrument gains more effectiveness as national economies become interdependent in the global economy. Therefore, this aspect of national power has increased as a way to influence another nation to do what we prefer.

A shortcoming with this option is that it can have adverse effects not only on the targeted country, but on the imposing country as well. Take, for example, again, the Iranians. They received economic sanctions, but they continued with their nuclear program because they were able to find other willing trade partners in Russia and China.

The third instrument is information. A nation can employ information in a variety of ways to sway opinion in a favorable direction. We used this instrument heavily in many of our past wars, undermining the resolve of enemy troops and populations by providing them with leaflets about our impending combat operations and the truth about their despotic regimes. Our enemies have used less ethical information operations against us. Remember Tokyo Rose? During World War II, she sent out Japanese propaganda over the radio to the Allied Forces who were conducting military operations in our campaign against the Japanese in the Pacific theater.

Moreover, I can give you a modern example of what the informational instrument looks like when used domestically in America. In fact, we are all "benefiting" from its effects right now. I'm talking about the information campaign currently employed by our own mostly leftist, mainstream media. Their usual mantra is that the illegal immigrant invasion we are currently experiencing causes no ill effects on Americans, and whoever disagrees with that is labeled a bigot, a racist or a xenophobe.

The informational instrument can be especially effective within our politically correct nation because all the mainstream media sources come out in force against any dissenter whenever the message does not conform to theirs. The bottom line, though, is that the informational instrument does not seem to have much effect on any other nations. Words are meaningless unless people receiving the message are receptive.

Finally, we have the military instrument of national power. Employment of the military option is typically the last resort of sane people. Take it from me—our combat forces are not chomping at the proverbial bit to get involved in a war. Now, don't get me wrong: We have the best-trained, best-led and best-equipped armed forces in the world. Nevertheless, warriors are not necessarily the ones who typically want to go to war because war has devastating costs. However, when it is the will of the American people, you can rely on America's combat forces to do their duty without equivocation.

There is also international opinion to consider when using the military. Many nations are victimized by and fraught with the opinions of the intellectual elite—those who are mortified by the thought of using lethal force. Overwhelming aversion to the use of force—in any instance—seems to permeate the international community. I agree that it is always more advantageous to attempt other measures before resorting to armed conflict, but how far are a rational people to be pushed before they have the natural right to exercise self-defense? For example, should America and her allies just sit back and allow rogue nations and non-state entities to run roughshod over them? Inaction is not in our national interest.

Even though military force is the alternative of last resort, it must be a key element of any grand strategy that we consider. In other words, as we have discussed, there are limitations when employing the instruments in isolation. Therefore, we have to consider what constitutes the most favorable combination of those options that are available to us.

For the sake of argument, let's say that there are nations that take deliberate actions to undermine our national interests in a certain part of the world—China, Russia and the majority of the Islamic world are prime examples. Depending on the specific set of circumstances, let's also assume that the situation is such that it presents an unacceptable threat to the welfare of our nation. Given this, it's logical that we would develop an integrated plan of action that takes advantage of the potential benefits from the application of diplomacy, economic sanctions, information operations and, at least, the threat of armed force.

Even though the military option should not be the first choice, it must always linger in the shadows as a possibility in order for the other instruments to have a chance of success. If we did not have the military that we have, how often would we be able to effect meaningful change in the world? Given the international climate and the dislike of the United States by many foreign governments, the answer is that there is little chance of us influencing any of the ruthless actors to our advantage. However, the good news is that this is not the case, and we should be willing to do what's required to ensure our national security.

Chapter Eighteen

The Military Decision-Making Process

Decision making is knowing if *to decide,*
then when, *and* what *to decide.*
—U.S. Army Field Manual 101-5, Staff Organization and Operations

The first order of business is to determine our objective regarding the exploitation of our country. We are under an assault by those who have no concern for our welfare or the stability of our nation. Those attacks are not well-coordinated, but they exist nonetheless and are led by foreign enemies against whom those of us in the military swore to defend our Constitution.

Not only are we under assault from those outside our borders, but also from some quarters within our own country. They are the domestic enemies we also gave an oath to oppose. Those forces believe that we should just have open borders and allow all comers to enter and let happen what may. This is an ill-conceived notion that, if left unchecked, would most certainty lead to our ruin—a total loss of our national identity and our common culture.

Cultural relativists would say that we are too harsh, and ask who we are to judge which culture is more deserving of existence than any other. I am not arguing which culture is better or worse. All I am saying is that I would prefer to live where and how I live now, with the cultural identity in which I grew up.

I have served and traveled in many parts of the world and I have experienced some wonderful places, but none is anything like what we have here in the United States. There are other wealthy nations, of course. However, there are also many nations that allow their people to live in abject poverty, which is really a shame, and no man who truly cares about others could ever just put these people out of his mind.

Many of us would like to avoid seeing these same conditions develop within our own nation. Consequently, I have included a detailed plan as to how the United States of America can defend its borders effectively. My focus is on our southern border because the situation on our northern border is entirely different, and may require a different solution. Nevertheless, the plan I have developed, unlike many other options being circulated by leftist and internationalist groups, provides the necessary elements that would actually do something substantive regarding this crisis.

How do we make a decision as to how best to solve the ills that are facing America from across our borders? Given the fact that many of the threats we face could be lethal, we should start looking at a military option that facilitates the self-defense of our nation. Such an approach, if adopted, would necessarily entail the employment of our armed forces to some extent—but would also be practical rather than simply politically expedient.

However, this proposal is more detailed than simply deploying troops to the scene generically. Rather, I want to take you through the entire decision-making process to determine an appropriate national response for the problems facing us. Once we get through this process, we will know to what extent we need to involve the military.

Before we get into the specific application of military planning principles, I want to take a few moments to talk you through what the Army calls the military decision-making process or MDMP. Before we dive into the meat of the proposal in the next chapter, my goal in this chapter is to explain where I am coming from.

As an added precursor to the discussion, I will briefly define the strategic, operational and tactical levels of war, as we will use these terms from this point on.

The strategic level of war:

> The level at which a nation…determines national security objectives and guidance, and develops and uses national resources to accomplish these objectives. Activities at this level establish national

> military objectives; sequence initiatives; define limits for the use of military and other instruments of national power; develop war plans to achieve these objectives; and provide military forces and other capabilities in accordance with strategic plans."[167]

The operational level of war:

> The level of war at which campaigns and major operations are planned, conducted, and sustained to accomplish strategic objectives within theaters or areas of operations. Activities at this level link tactics and strategy by establishing operational objectives needed to accomplish the strategic objectives, sequencing events to achieve the operational objectives, initiating actions, and applying resources to bring about and sustain these events. These activities provide the means to ensure that tactical successes are exploited to achieve strategic objectives.[168]

The tactical level of war:

> The level of war at which battles and engagements are planned and executed to accomplish military objectives assigned to tactical units or task forces. Activities at this level focus on the ordered arrangement and maneuver of combat elements in relation to each other and to the enemy to achieve combat objectives.[169]

I will present an abridged version of the process. This will facilitate understanding of the methodology of what we need do in defense of our country's borders.

First, let's look at the set methodology applied to military planning.

The military decision-making process is a single, established, and proven analytical process… The MDMP helps the commander and his staff examine a battlefield situation and reach logical conclusions. The process helps them apply thoroughness, clarity, sound judgment, logic, and professional knowledge to reach a decision.[170]

The MDMP is comprised of seven steps:

1. Receipt of mission
2. Mission analysis
3. Course of action development
4. Course of action analysis
5. Course of action comparison
6. Course of action approval
7. Orders production

In step one, receipt of mission, the National Command Authorities (NCA—the president and the secretary of defense) direct that the armed forces take certain actions in support of national objectives. Some examples are the Granada Invasion, the Panama Invasion, Desert Shield/Desert Storm and, most recently, the invasions of Afghanistan and Iraq as part of the global war on terrorism. In each of these campaigns, the NCA defined strategic objectives for the armed forces to accomplish in what is commonly referred to as a "directive."

Once the NCA issues a directive to the appropriate combatant commander, that commander then "issue[s] a planning directive that provides essential planning guidance and directs the initiation of execution planning before the directing authority approves a military course of action"[171] (COA). Execution planning is based on an NCA-approved COA that is translated into an actual plan or operation order that would be executed by an appropriate field commander.[172]

The service departments may also receive this directive so they can begin their planning processes, as appropriate, to support the development of the combatant commander's campaign plan. Then, within each of the services, at each command echelon, the appropriate commander develops plans to complement the campaign plan that, in the end, translates strategic objectives into operational objectives and operational objectives into tactical objectives.

During the process of translation of operational to tactical objectives, each echelon of command has to tailor its specific tasks to enable the accomplishment of the higher commander's tasks. In the end, the tactical actions of even an infantry fire team (five or so soldiers on the battlefield) are linked, through the various command echelons, to the original directive issued by the NCA.

To help put this process into the perspective of a well-known military campaign, let's look at the ongoing campaign in Afghanistan. In very simplistic terms, we were attacked by al-Qaeda on September 11, 2001, so the NCA directed that the then-commander, Central Command (CENTCOM) General Tommy Franks, destroy al-Qaeda in Afghanistan. The planning echelons within CENTCOM and other designated supporting federal agencies went to work to develop the appropriate plans and orders that led to the destruction of much of the al-Qaeda network in Afghanistan.

You may recall seeing footage of our soldiers fighting on the ground and our air forces dropping ordnance on certain targets. These battlefield activities were planned and synchronized to carry out the original directive issued by the NCA.

Step two in the process is mission analysis. As each command echelon receives its orders, they are analyzed to determine exactly what the mission should be for that subordinate command echelon in order to facilitate the higher commander's mission accomplishment. They then decide which orders they will send down to their subordinate command echelons.

Mission analysis specifically defines the who (the specific unit), the what (the tactical task—attack, defend, etc.—and its purpose), the where (the area of operations in which the unit is to accomplish its mission), the when (the start time of the operation) and the why (the purpose of the operation within the context of the greater whole) of a command's actions.

An example of a mission statement might be: "On 250600NOV2006 (when—the twenty-fifth day of November, 2006, at 6:00 a.m.), 1st Cavalry Division (who) defends from [grid coordinates that define the division's area of operations (AO)] (where) to deny the enemy any penetration of the U.S.-Mexico border (what or task), so as to facilitate the security of the United States against drug traffickers, terrorists, illegal immigrants and slave traders (why or purpose)."

The cleaned up version would be: "On 250600NOV2006, 1st Cavalry Division defends from AZ 3256 to AZ 5763 to BD 4817 to BD 3521 to deny the enemy any penetration of the U.S.-Mexico border, so as to facilitate the security of the United States against drug traffickers, terrorists, illegal immigrants and slave traders."

When a commander receives his orders, he determines his mission statement and then sends orders to his subordinate units that, once accomplished, will facilitate the accomplishment of his mission.

Step three is course of action (COA) development. There are many ways to accomplish a mission, and this is when the planners put forward some options, describing how his unit can accomplish its assigned mission, for a commander to choose. This planning phase usually ends when there are at least three friendly COAs and three enemy COAs. These are then used for analysis in the next step.

Step four is course of action analysis. During this planning step, the planners take the COAs, or planning options, and "war-game" them against what they estimate will be the threat that our forces will face. In short, they walk through the anticipated operation on a map board or terrain board, using appropriate symbols for the units, and determine whether the COAs are decisive, achievable and doable. This process is often referred to as "action-reaction-counteraction."

For example, in planning an offensive operation, we would move a unit forward on the board (our action); the opposing forces would move on the board in response to our action (the enemy's reaction); and then we would again take action (our counteraction). This entire process is designed to ensure that we have the necessary assets and capabilities available to accomplish the mission and to begin the process of synchronizing the military's complex systems in space, time and purpose.

In step five, course of action comparison, the planners compare the COAs against each other according to agreed-upon decision criteria. Some of these criteria might be unity of effort, mass or supportability. If there are three COAs, then the planners compare COAs one and two, COAs one and three, and COAs two and three, each done in isolation. Following this analysis, the planners assess the advantages and disadvantages of each COA to determine which is the best option.

The planners' findings are often portrayed to the commander in the form of a decision matrix that compares all of the COAs based on the decision criteria. Moreover, each criterion is usually assigned a weight because they are not all typically equal in importance.

In step six, course of action approval, the commander makes his decision as to which COA he will use. He can approve a COA as-is, or he can give guidance that modifies a COA into what he wants.

Step seven calls for orders production. This is when the operations planners take what the commander decides, turn it into the appropriate orders, and then disseminate those orders as necessary to the subordinate commanders, as noted in step two above.

It is important to understand that no matter how detailed a plan may appear, there will always be the need for adjustments to the base plan once the shooting starts. However, rigorous prior planning should serve to reduce the emergence of unforeseen, decisive enemy actions. Carl von Clausewitz, in his masterpiece *On War*, defines this condition as the "friction of war."[173]

Chapter Nineteen

Plans Development

Given the evidence presented, can you now agree that we are in a war on many fronts? In the global war on terror (GWOT), we are confronting those who want to kill us in a more blatantly obvious war than the one coming to us primarily from Mexico, Central America and much of the southern half of the Western Hemisphere.

In the previous chapter, the military decision-making process methodology was presented to enable a more detailed analysis beginning in this chapter. We will use the MDMP methodology to arrive at a framework for a federal solution to counter the threats against the United States. In doing so, I will use the steps discussed earlier, adding appropriate details to apply that same methodology to our current situation.

By the time we finish, I will have provided a course of action that, with further analysis by the appropriate joint force commander (JFC), Congress and the president, should facilitate planning for and conduct of the decisive actions that our country must take if we are serious about defending ourselves.

A joint force commander, in the context of our analysis, is the combatant commander authorized to exercise combatant command (command authority) over a joint force.[174] A joint force is comprised of two or more military departments operating under a single JFC.[175] Since our situation would require Army, Air Force and naval forces, the combatant commander would also be designated as the joint force commander.

Given the anticipated complexity of operations, there is a need for the designation of military-department-specific JFCs—namely a joint force land component commander (JFLCC), a joint force air component commander (JFACC), a joint force maritime component commander (JFMCC) and a joint force special operations component commander (JFSOCC), as well as others as deemed appropriate. These commanders will work for the JFC and facilitate the planning, coordination and execution of operations in support of the JFC's overall campaign plan.

The good news is that the command and control infrastructure that we require is already in place in the United States Southern Command (USSOUTHCOM, also referred to as SOUTHCOM). We already have in place what we need to get started immediately on defending our nation.

In addition to the MDMP steps defined earlier, I will add details that are specific to our border situation. I will focus on the main threats—drug traffickers and human traffickers—because if we succeed against these we can be confident that other threats will be defeated in the process. I will also provide a possible directive for the NCA to issue to the appropriate combatant commander and put forward a possible mission statement for the designated JFC, who will be expected to carry out the appropriate campaign planning necessary to drive the formulation of subordinate unit plans and orders.

In our situation, the first action that must be taken is the issuance of an appropriate directive by the NCA to an appropriate combatant commander. At minimum, such a directive should include the strategic objectives that, through the application of the military instrument of national power, would be accomplished. Such a directive should include:

1. Deploy such forces as necessary (air, land and sea) to defend the U.S.-Mexico border and deny any penetration thereof from south of the border.
2. Conduct cross-border operations as necessary to destroy the threats and their associated supporting systems that enable their illegal activities to affect the United States adversely.

3. Define the area of operation (AO) in which the JFC is to accomplish his assigned mission.

For the purpose of defining responsibilities, I will designate the JFC as the commander in chief of Southern Command (CINCSOUTHCOM). The current mission of SOUTHCOM includes deterring and defeating transnational threats to the United States—a mission statement that is compatible with our border defense objectives.

To begin with, a possible directive from the NCA might look something like the following:

> Effective immediately, CINCSOUTHCOM assumes command of air, land and sea forces, as designated by the secretary of defense and with support from designated federal agencies, to defend the U.S.-Mexico border and to deny any penetration of that border by the adversaries of the United States, which include drug traffickers, terrorists, human traffickers and illegal immigrants, so as to preserve law and order and the sovereignty of the United States. Once the border is secure, continue operations as necessary to interdict and destroy the threats and their associated support systems that enable illegal activities to affect adversely the United States.
>
> Your area of operations will be from a line that is approximately twenty-five miles to the north of and generally runs parallel to the U.S.-Mexico border. Your AO consists of those countries to our south that are enablers of the illegal activities that have permeated much of Mexico, Central America, South America, nations in the Caribbean and the associated sea and air lanes throughout the Caribbean Sea, the Gulf of Mexico, the western Atlantic Ocean and the eastern Pacific Ocean. At end-state, the illegal drug trafficking networks will no longer be able to export their illegal drugs into the United States; the illegal human trafficking network, including illegal immigrants, will no longer be able to facilitate the illegal entry of foreign nationals into the United States; and terrorist attempts to enter our country and all other forms of illegal activity will be ineffective at exploiting the citizenry of the United States.

Chapter Twenty

MDMP Applied

Since the commander of SOUTHCOM (cdr, SOUTHCOM) is to be the combatant commander for this analysis, he would be designated the joint force commander. In keeping with the planning processes, he would receive the directive cited earlier, along with any additional planning guidance.

The next step is for the cdr, SOUTHCOM and his staff to perform mission analysis. Since he would conduct joint operations, his organization would also have the appropriate military department representatives mentioned previously, which include JFLCC, JFACC, JFMCC and JFSOCC.

Next comes the mission analysis. During this step, the staff sections begin to formulate initial estimates of how much each would contribute to the upcoming campaign—including operations, intelligence, engineer, logistics and so on. However, we will focus on the mission statement and definition of the battlefield framework that the operations section produces and the initial stages of the intelligence and engineer estimates, which are closely linked in the determination of the fence/barrier systems (engineer component) and the analysis of the terrain (intelligence component).

The operations estimate, on the other hand, considers all elements that can influence the unit's current operations and feasible future operations. It results in a recommendation to the commander.

When beginning to plan something like this, some considerations have to be taken into account. Toward that end I want to dedicate some attention to the fundamental distinction between two terms: security and defense. We typically refer to operations along our borders as "security" because law enforcement is proficient at that—in the law enforcement sense. Nonetheless, what we are talking about along our borders requires more. These operations require the defense of our nation's border.

In the military sense the term "security" means something somewhat different than the law enforcement sense. In military operations, security is an inherent task for any commander in that he must protect his forces from surprise, attack or some other disruptive action that an adversary may be able to bring to bear on them. So, we are trying to provide security to the nation to counter the threats we face.

However, we must be committed enough to array those forces required to defend our nation from this invasion. As mentioned several times throughout our discussion, we are in a war. Therefore, in military terms, defense of our borders is required and not just security. Nonetheless, security operations would be an aspect of the overall defensive posture that we should assume along our border with Mexico.

We must also consider the fact that, except in extremely rare occasions, defense is not decisive. In other words, we will not win the war we are facing unless we are willing to use offensive operations in coordination with any defensive plan that we may ultimately devise. The offense is the decisive form of military operations, and it can lead to victory. We can achieve many of our objectives only if we address our problem with full force rather than just at the half step because we do not want to offend anybody.

It is to our advantage that the threats we face right now are less than fully coordinated. Nevertheless, we need integrated operations to counter these things that harm our country and our people. One reason why is that we have been trying to disrupt some of those forces—such as the interdiction operations associated with our nation's war on drugs—but we are not striking against the transnational drug organizations in a thorough and decisive manner. In other words, we are not attacking these organizations in depth. By stopping their ability to move their illicit drugs across our southern border, we would potentially be better able to attack their systems with greater magnitude.

An example might be an operation in connection with the war on drugs in which we defend the border (in all dimensions—land, air, and sea) and conduct offensive operations to eradicate illicit-drug-related crops, engage and destroy the armed forces that support those drug-related operations, and interdict air, land and sea transshipment lanes to deny the enemy their use.

Once we conduct these operations for a while, assuredly the opposition would begin to feel the heat. However, we must be willing to go all the way, or it would be a waste of time because it would just go on and on with no real end—similar to what is happening with our current approach to the drug war. Our operations are not completely futile, but they will never be decisive until we cut off the supply of drugs to the distributors and users in coordination with the eradication of the supporting infrastructure in the respective source countries.

Once the initial considerations are examined, we can move on to the mission statement, which would be similar to the NCA directive I detailed at the end of the last chapter.

MISSION STATEMENT

On order, SOUTHCOM deploys air, land, and sea forces to the vicinity of the U.S.-Mexico border to establish a defense of the U.S.-Mexico border and to deny any penetration of that border by the adversaries of the United States, including drug traffickers, terrorists, human traffickers, and illegal immigrants, so as to preserve law and order and to preserve the sovereignty of the United States. SOUTHCOM's AO begins in the north, along a line that is approximately twenty-five miles to the north of and generally runs parallel to the U.S.-Mexico border and then encompasses those countries to our south that are enablers of the illegal activities that have permeated much of Mexico, Central America, South America, many nations in the Caribbean, and the associated sea and air lanes throughout the Caribbean Sea, Gulf of Mexico, the Western Atlantic Ocean, and the Eastern Pacific Ocean. (Note that there are many possible variants to this mission statement that may be just as effective, but what we have defined will suffice for the purposes of this discussion.)

Once the mission statement is in place, the battlefield framework can be laid. "[The] battlefield framework helps commanders relate friendly forces to one another and to the enemy in terms of time, space, and purpose."[176] There are many aspects to a commander's AO, but we will confine our discussion, for the sake of brevity, to the *deep*, *close* and *rear* operations areas.

Let me give an example of these as they apply to our current global war on terror. Simply put, from a strategic perspective, the interior of the United

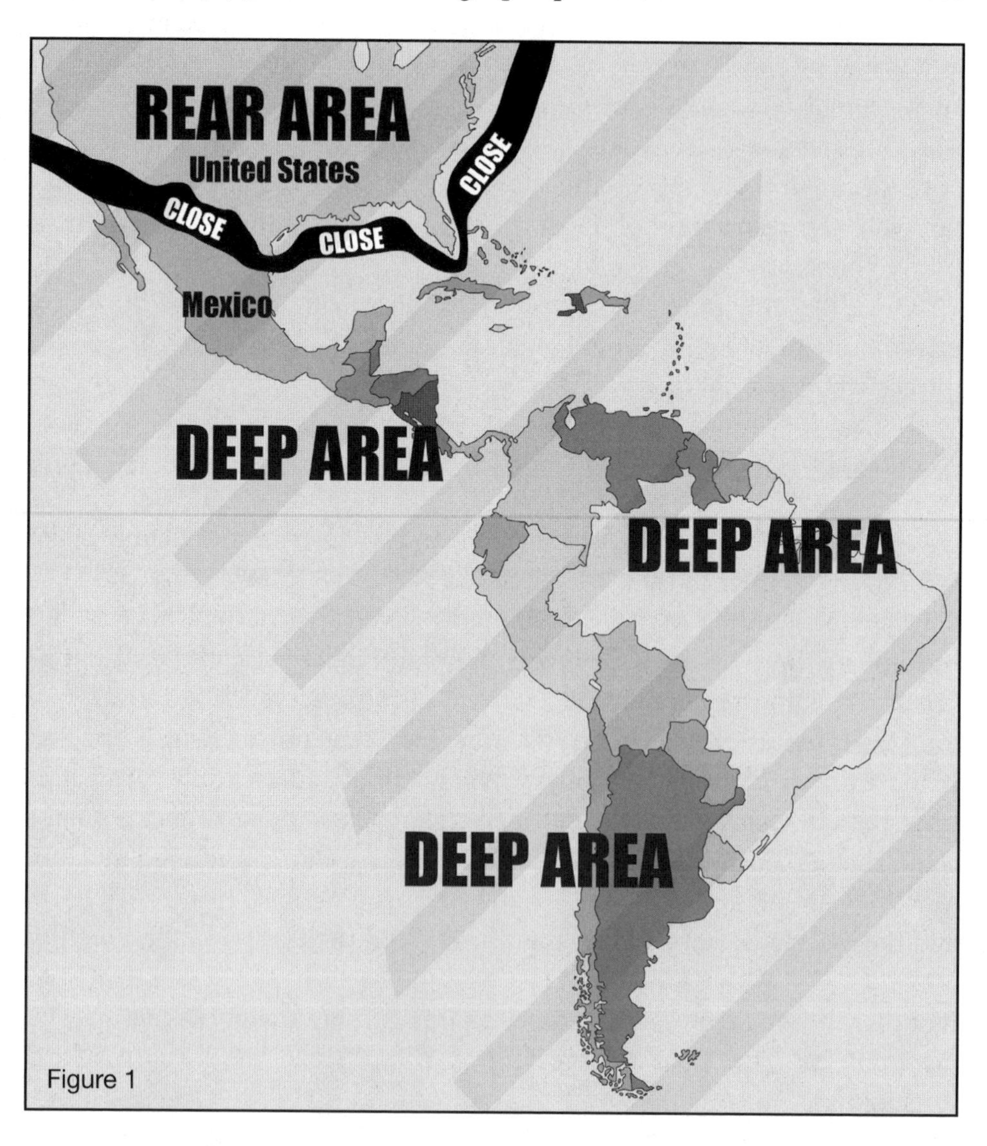

Figure 1

States is the rear area; terrorists attacked us in this area when they flew airliners into the World Trade Center towers. Operations in Iraq and Afghanistan are examples of the deep area, since these operations are "over there." And our operations to defend our borders are aspects of what can be defined as the "close" area of operations.

Considering the example presented above, from an operational perspective, SOUTHCOM's close operations area would generally be where our forces defend along the U.S.-Mexico border and our coastlines; the deep operations area would generally be to the south of the continental U.S.; and the rear operations area would generally be within the limits of the United States. (See Figure 1.)

It's important to identify these operating areas in order to facilitate the arrangement of battlefield activities in time, space and purpose throughout the entire AO. I mentioned two examples of battlefield activities previously—soldiers fighting on the ground and air forces dropping ordnance on certain targets.

Here, our "deep" area is generally south of the United States and expands into areas of interest that would, at minimum, encompass the Caribbean Sea, Mexico, Central America, well into South America and the surrounding sea lanes. In the war on terror, the deep area is literally global and I believe that we are tracking all associated terror threats as is required for our national security. The president is resolute in the war on terror, so I will not spend time on this aspect of our anticipated deep area. For our discussion, the deep area is defined based on our capability to acquire and counter threats against the sovereignty of America that originate or transit through the area.

So, in summary: The threats are currently concentrated in and around Mexico because there is little effective resistance on the part of the United States at its border. As we begin to counter the current, primary avenues of approach into our country, threats will naturally begin to seek out alternative routes to maintain their stranglehold on their operations in and around the U.S.

Our close area of operations is generally along our borders. This is the area in which we must stand and counter the illegal entrants into our country and the other illegal undertakings of transnational criminal organizations.

In this case, since we are describing what amounts to a defensive military operation, this would be the general area in which we would defend our country.

Our rear area consists of the internal areas of our country. If there are elements of illegal operations within our rear area, law enforcement must take appropriate countermeasures.

Given all this, what we have to accomplish and the area in which we must operate seems quite daunting. But if the United States is serious about its difficulties, we will be up to the task.

We must now determine what the situation is as it relates to our mission and create our intelligence estimate. In military planning, we define the friendly forces available for employment and lay out the opposing forces that we must counter in order to accomplish our given mission. As for identifying the enemy, we have several of them arrayed against us. We know of slave traders, drug traffickers, Islamic terrorists, illegal immigrants, criminals fleeing justice and potential carriers of infectious diseases. There are probably others, but this list will do for the purposes of this discussion.

Of course, we also need to analyze our adversaries. One aspect we must understand is that they are not conducting an in-your-face, frontal assault. Instead, they are infiltrating our country secretly and silently.

It is also an important part of the intelligence estimate to analyze the five military aspects of terrain so that we know how to make maximum use of it. We must use the topography to our advantage to counter the threats.

The five military aspects of terrain considered in the military planning process are represented by the acronym OKOCA, which stands for:

O: observation and fields of fire
K: key and decisive terrain
O: existing obstacles—natural and manmade
C: cover and concealment
A: avenues of approach of the threat(s).

We can apply a similar methodology to the operations needed to secure our border.

The results of terrain analysis will assist in determining where we can best employ our forces and capabilities to counter those of the enemy. During this analysis, we identify the avenues that the enemies would most likely use in order to enter our country illegally. We already know that they use land, air and sea approaches to gain access to America, but we would define avenues specifically so we could deploy forces to stop the illegal entries into America more effectively and efficiently.

Next comes the threat forces estimate. In considering the threats, there are those who are typically nonviolent, such as immigrants attempting to enter illegally, and the violent variety such as drug traffickers, terrorists and possibly those who bring in the illegal immigrants. Obviously, the idea is to deal with each appropriately.

First, we must determine how many there are in each category. Glancing at the news reveals tens of thousands of illegal immigrants attempting to enter our country, thousands of drug traffickers operating in and around the United States, countless terrorists and people with infectious diseases—and the statistics we have clearly indicate that these groups are increasing in size. The threat certainly looks overwhelming, but let me emphasize that we can and must prevail.

In evaluating the dangers arrayed against us, we have to take into account how the various threats operate and where they tend to enter our country, as well as the geography of those areas. Some examples might be the drug traffickers who repeatedly enter through the Laredo, Texas, area or the San Diego, California, area. Given the geography of these two locales, it would not take much time for an illicit-drug trafficker to travel the relatively short distance required to get far enough into our country and practically disappear into the urban landscape. It becomes more difficult for law enforcement to find him once he reaches an urban environment. In this situation, I recommend a substantial, fixed barrier that is difficult to breach, complemented with electronic early-warning devices, surveillance systems and a guard force to counter any attempts at illegal entry.

Since the war on drugs and the war on illegal immigration are two major threats against which we must defend ourselves, I will briefly discuss how to begin the process of creating a unified vision and resulting plan of action to counter these two threats. Through this analysis, we will be able to focus scarce resources on the war on drugs and the war on illegal immigration. If we can defeat these two basic threats, we can potentially reduce the effects of other threats.

In combating the illicit drugs that continue to flow into America, we should focus on six primary components of the overall illegal-drug trade:

1. cultivation and harvesting (supply)
2. processing into product
3. transshipment
4. distribution
5. users of illegal drugs (demand)
6. money laundering

For the reasons outlined in the discussion of corruption in the Western Hemisphere (see Appendix II), we must go after the first two components of the drug trade primarily in Bolivia, Colombia, Mexico and Venezuela.

The most significant transshipment areas for the movement of illicit drugs *en route* to the United States are Aruba, the Bahamas, Barbados, Belize, British Virgin Islands, Costa Rica, Dominican Republic, Guyana, Haiti, Jamaica, Honduras, Mexico and Panama.

Of course, the United States is where the distribution and user components exist.

The money laundering centers of component six are Aruba, Brazil, Colombia, Dominican Republic, Guyana, Haiti, Jamaica, Panama, Venezuela and the United States.

When we review the operational environment and the location of the various countries involved, we can begin to envision where we need to focus our counter drug-related operations. We can also see which countries participate in one or more of the illicit drug-related components. (See Figure 2.)

In discussing the combat of illegal immigration in the deep areas, I am going to assume that there is a correlation between the deportable immigrants we do catch and the countries from which they originate. Through this analysis, we should be able to determine on which countries we should focus our efforts—hopefully using diplomatic and economic means—to

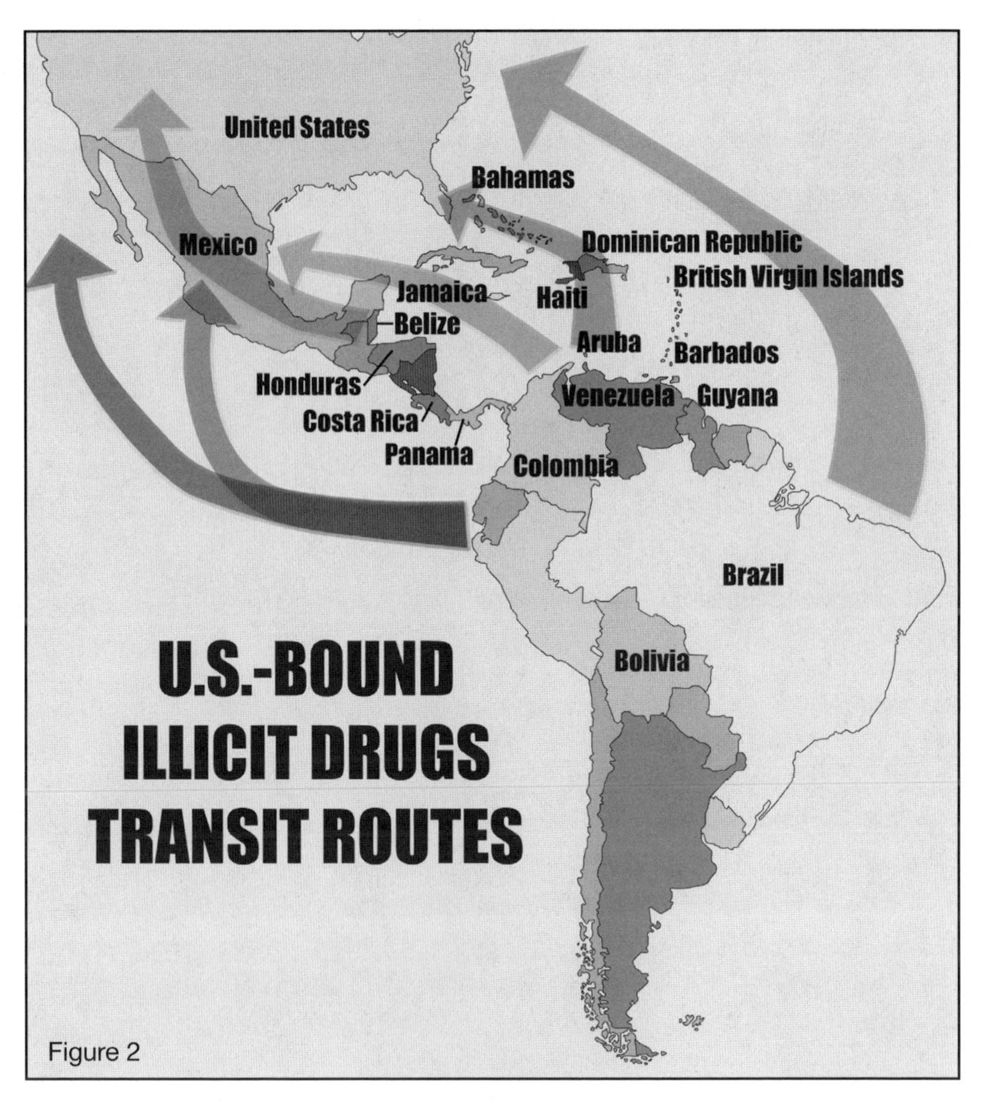

Figure 2

reduce their people's desire to leave their countries and come to the United States.

According to the *Yearbook of Immigration Statistics: 2007*,[177] the major source countries for illegal immigrants measured by Border Patrol apprehensions and Immigration and Customs Enforcement arrests are:

1. Mexico: 854,261
2. Honduras: 28,263

3. Guatemala: 23,907
4. El Salvador: 19,699
5. Cuba: 4,932

Worlwide Total: 960,756

The numbers for the next source country fall considerably, so we should focus primarily on the countries I have listed.

Chapter Twenty-One

The Fence Question

Next I will address the engineer estimate because the plan coordination that occurs among the operations planners, the intelligence planners and the engineer planners will result in a barrier plan that will complement the cdr, SOUTHCOM's overall campaign plan. First I will describe some of the military planning that precedes decisions regarding the use of barriers.

There has been talk in the media about whether or not we should place a fence or wall along our entire southern border with Mexico, which is approximately 2,000 miles long. However, there are several points to keep in mind as we consider this option. First, the leadership of this country must realize that we have severe problems with many of our neighbors in the Western Hemisphere—and that those problems primarily result from our nation's failed policy that keeps our southern border open. It is, essentially, an open border because it is no more effective than a sieve.

Second, we must "pin the rose" on one individual to be responsible for operations that are designed to seal our border with Mexico (for example, commander, SOUTHCOM). Third, that one individual must develop a plan to keep any and all invaders from coming into our country via our border.

It is only at this point, during the planning process, that we can determine the utility of using a barrier system and make provisions for its employment because it is dependent on the overall campaign plan. It is foolish to build a plan on the assumed premise that we should have a fence along our entire border with Mexico—much less predetermine what kind of fence that would be. The issue as to whether or not we should have a fixed barrier is not answerable with a simple "yes" or "no." The issue is much larger and more complex than that.

When I was in the military, when we planned an operation, we considered all the assets and capabilities we had available to accomplish our assigned mission. Considering barriers and obstacles, they can take many forms:

- Gap (wet or dry)
- Concertina wire (commonly referred to as barbed wire)
- Logjam, abatis, fence, wall, etc.

Fundamentally, in order to increase the propensity for success we should employ a proper mix of capabilities instead of basing an operation on any single capability—especially when we consider that there are different types of terrain along our 2,000-mile border with Mexico.

The need for a fence on our border depends on what the overall national plan of action is to defend our nation. At present, we have not developed a clearly defined plan of action. However, over the next several chapters I will put forward a viable plan for the defense of our country. If America implements a similar plan, it would be necessary to use barriers and obstacles.

Regarding the fence debate, there are proponents who want to leverage technology and erect a virtual fence. Others comment that we must have a wall, and nothing short of that will suffice.

Sensors are an option, but their viability depends on our ability to respond to a threat once it sets off an alarm. It is not efficient to allow a sensor to indicate an intrusion and then spend time and manpower to find the violators on our side of the border. Our border agents and internal enforcement agents already expend an inordinate amount of time and resources locating, detaining, processing and making appropriate disposition of violators—not to mention the drain on state resources.

Another drawback of using mostly high-tech methods is that these systems are subject to damage by those attempting the illegal actions. Do you think that drug cartels are going to say, "Oh, well, they have sensors, so we cannot go this way"? I think not. It's more likely that the organized criminals would develop ways to counter our sensor systems and move through anyway.

In addition, repeated destruction of sensor systems can become very costly very quickly. For the companies that supply the systems, this is good news. But for the taxpayers who fund this project and expect results, this is certainly not a great idea.

Before we make an educated decision on the issue of a fence on our border with Mexico, let's spend a few moments trying to understand the purpose of a barrier system in any form. Again, because of my experience in the military, I tend to place the border defense issue into a military planner's context. So when people talk about border protection and a need for a fence, the first thing I envision in my mind is an appropriate barrier plan that would complement the efforts of the United States to defend its border.

As we begin to look at the option of a barrier, we must first realize that any barrier, no matter how imposing it may be, is not a stand-alone solution in and of itself. Any type of barrier plan, whether it be a fixed structure or an electronic early warning system—the virtual fence—must have "eyes on." A barrier that is not under observation, either electronically or by a person, is next to useless. In other words, we cannot place a barrier in the area and think that is the solution to all of our problems.

The purpose of a barrier is to control, deter, impede or otherwise slow down a person's or vehicle's ability to gain unwanted access to a particular area. A prison is an obvious example of this because it has barriers—typically walls and fencing—designed to impede the unwanted exit of criminals from the facility. On the other hand, prisons also have guards who respond to escape attempts because a prison wall by itself will not necessarily keep the prisoners in a prison. Likewise, a prison without a physical wall—with only a guard force—would be manpower-intensive to secure, much like an electronic barrier would be at the border. Electronic early-warning systems can be excellent security multipliers, but without some degree of fixed barrier, the manpower requirement would necessarily increase. Add to this the fact that the well-financed drug cartels already have a history of obtaining high-tech weaponry and countermeasures and you can readily see how short-lived any initial success of a virtual barrier would be.

So we can see that there is a correlation between the use of a barrier and early-warning systems and the need for manpower. At one extreme is a solid barrier that requires much less manpower; at the other, there is no man-made obstruction but the need for manpower increases. We might want to consider some mix that maximizes the advantages of fixed barriers, early-warning systems and manpower. In other words, there may be more to the issue than just a one-size-fits-all approach to the entire length of our border with Mexico.

There appear to be two limits to the operational environment within which our border forces would have to operate. At the one end are the urban environments adjacent to the border, and at the other end are the much–less-populated desert areas that adjoin the border. At first glance, this signals that the tactics we use to defend the border in a built-up area would not be the same tactics we would use to defend the less-populated desert areas.

In the context of border defense, the purposes of a barrier would be to control the access of people who are allowed access to the United States (e.g., legal immigrants) and deter and impede those who are not allowed free access to our country (e.g., terrorists, drug traffickers, human traffickers, etc.). By giving the commander, SOUTHCOM the mission to defend our southern border, much of the debate surrounding the merits of a border "wall" would be moot since once a commander receives the mission, he would define the need for a system of obstacles as an inherent part of his overall campaign plan. The military already has the staff sections and skills to prepare a barrier plan based on what is required to defend our border.

Now, we turn our attention to our final determination in this mission analysis: the friendly forces estimate. Given what we're facing, the next step is to assess what forces and capabilities we must array and then employ in order to counter the threats. As the only remaining world superpower, our forces are many and varied, so I will not attempt to cite each one. However, some of the major players are the Department of State, the Department of Homeland Security, the Department of Defense (both active and reserve components), the FBI, the DEA, the CIA, the Centers for Disease Control and Prevention, and state, local and tribal law enforcement agencies.

There is an indispensable principle upon which we should anchor our strategy: the concept of synergy, which is a way of orchestrating and synchronizing operations to leverage the effects of the whole, in comparison to attempting to rely on the parts that make up that whole. In other words, with synergy we stand to leverage a whole that is greater than the sum of its parts.

We keep hearing from various circles that we must commit to enforcing the laws within our own borders or that we must secure the border—and, sometimes, people propose a combination of the two. A combination of both internal enforcement and defense of our border *is* essential, but this alone would not accomplish our goal. Any course of action that does not include pressure in our deep area would not be successful, because we would constantly be in reaction mode against whatever the threats threw at us.

Even in the global war on terror, our nation easily determined that it was much better to take the war to the enemies' home turf than to fight them on our own soil. This is an excellent example of deep operations, and we need to have that same mindset with regard to drug cartels and human traffickers. Thus, we must conduct operations that contribute to our overall success in all areas—the deep, the close and the rear.

Moreover, the close area of our border has been widely ignored by the Bush administration. This is a serious strategic error on the part of our president and his advisers given the recent upsurge of Arabic infiltrators into our nation from Mexico, as reported by sheriff departments in the border areas. Would it not be better to prevent these people from getting in and taxing our rear-area assets in their efforts to prevent terrorist attacks? This may seem like an insurmountable task, but it can be accomplished through an important principle of war known as "unity of effort." This translates in part to the focusing of necessary, available assets in a timely and efficient manner—in time, space, and purpose—in the overall campaign.

Chapter Twenty-Two

Course of Action Development

Our next step is to develop potential courses of action for resolving the border crisis. Courses of action are to be decisive, achievable and doable—otherwise known as "DAD."

In developing our courses of action, we need to go back and take a look at our mission, review the threats and determine our capabilities to counter those threats. Actual COAs would be much more detailed than those presented in this chapter, but I will identify the major highlights of some potential COAs.

Course of action #1: the "feel-good" option. A first option typically contemplated during the COA development process is doing nothing—or, in this case, continuing with the *status quo*. We can see that our Republican leadership is currently employing that option at just about all levels of government; what a shame. S.2611 pretty much outlines this COA because it does nothing but make our situation worse.

I have to also mention that the Democrats are not doing anything either. It seems that almost all politicians are willing to keep pointing their fingers somewhere other than at themselves, rather than actually enacting legislation that addresses our crisis.

Course of action #2: the "we are really going to get serious now!" option. In this second option more manpower is added in the form of increased

Border Patrol officers augmented with National Guard assets (in support roles only) in the meantime. At the same time, we continue to carry out internal security operations and enforce immigration laws as we have been attempting to do for many years. Lastly, we hire more government bureaucrats and throw billions and billions more dollars at the situation. Apparently, the public often believes that there is real improvement when the government says that it's spending more money on something, when in reality there may be little or no correlation between increased spending and positive results.

Course of action #3: the "decisive action" option. Here we follow the concept briefly discussed earlier. This option calls for twelve steps:

1. Recognize the fact that we are in a war for our very existence and our very way of life.
2. Realign the areas of responsibility (AORs) of SOUTHCOM and U.S. Northern Command (NORTHCOM) so that SOUTHCOM has responsibility for the deep, close and rear areas as defined in Figure 1. Establish an appropriate command relationship between the commander, NORTHCOM and the commander, SOUTHCOM (with the commander, SOUTHCOM as the supported commander.)
3. Assign the commander, SOUTHCOM the task of defending the United States, with an assigned area of operations that includes our border with Mexico, the Gulf of Mexico, the Caribbean Sea, appropriate portions of the Atlantic and Pacific Oceans and specific regions of Central America, South America and Mexico and the adjacent sea areas, as required.
4. Tailor ground forces so as to provide the commander, SOUTHCOM the resources and capabilities necessary to accomplish his assigned task and purpose.
5. Increase the end-strength of our armed forces by 44,000 to 50,000 soldiers (primarily composed of United States Army combat arms soldiers) and place these assets under the commander, SOUTHCOM.
6. Task-organize sea and air assets as necessary under the commander, SOUTHCOM, so he has the assets and capabilities that

are necessary to accomplish his assigned task and purpose.

7. Erect an appropriate barrier along the entire southwestern border of the United States as determined by the commander, SOUTHCOM.
8. Establish an appropriate support relationship between the director, Homeland Security, and the commander, SOUTHCOM (with the commander, SOUTHCOM, as the supported commander).
9. Establish coordination and support relationships, as required, between the appropriate federal agencies and the commander, SOUTHCOM (again, SOUTHCOM is the supported commander for all assigned operations).
10. Commander, SOUTHCOM develops his campaign plan, gains approval from the commander in chief and executes the campaign plan. At minimum, one of his essential tasks must be to defend (seal) our southwestern border and all other sea and air routes of ingress into the United States.
11. The United States government conducts diplomatic, economic and informational operations that complement the overall military campaign plan.
12. Congress passes appropriate immigration legislation that maximizes entry based on merit and that maintains our culture and national identity.

Chapter Twenty-Three

MDMP: The Final Steps

Now that we have our courses of action, it's time to define the decision criteria that we will use in our analysis. There are additional factors, but for the purpose of this analysis, let's consider the following criteria:

1. Cost
2. Unity of command
3. Unity of effort
4. Efficient use of resources (taxpayer dollars)
5. Manpower
6. Effect on the U.S. economy
7. Use of the instruments of national power
8. Public opinion
9. International opinion

Now, let's look at our course of action options and weigh the pros and cons of each.

COA #1: THE "FEEL-GOOD" OPTION

Advantages: Continuing along this path appears to save the federal government money because the actual *costs* are diluted across many states. They will bear the brunt of the financial burden—and will continue to do so under this COA. The issue of *manpower* could show some economies of scale, but when efficiencies are measured, that may not be the case. This course of action will play well in the arena of *international opinion* because it allows the occurrence of illegal activities to continue in the Western Hemisphere, and many around the world believe that it is the responsibility of the "rich" Americans to prop up the rest of the world.

Disadvantages: *Unity of command* and *unity of effort* are not fully implemented under this option. There are attempts at orchestrating certain tasks through the DHS, FBI, CIA, DEA, CDC, etc., but there are many agencies (federal, state, local and tribal) that are pulled in different directions. One direction entails accomplishing job-related tasks and the other is the added responsibility to support the director, Homeland Security and other federal initiatives.

The current alignment is one of cooperation as opposed to one of clearly defined duties and responsibilities. Unity of command and effort are inextricably linked to the *efficient use of resources*; as unity declines so does efficiency. This option does not take advantage of our nation's instruments of national power.

It appears that the focus of our *informational instrument* is to condemn all attempts to correct the situation rather than to inform Americans of the extent and severity of our situation. We are using our *economic instrument* in an inefficient manner that does not lift up the economic levels in the countries that we are attempting to assist—there is some improvement, but corruption, in many of them, is an almost insurmountable inhibitor of our good intentions. Often, when we send aid to other countries, the money never makes it to its intended destination and ends up in the hands of corrupt government officials and other criminals.

Our *diplomatic instrument* continues to be used in such a way as to realize no real substantive results, but we throw money at the problem and attempt to "nice" other countries into submission. We are not making much use of our *military instrument* in the critical areas and continue to relegate it to the continued partnerships, joint exercises and so on that we have with certain suspect countries, all in an effort to build "meaningful relationships."

The *effect on the U.S. economy* will continue to be corrosive. The American taxpayer and many businesses carry a tax burden that prevents the accumulation of wealth to support additional economic prosperity and expansion. Many Americans desire to maintain our national identity, culture and way of life. Based on my survey of voters and recent national polling data, this option would not go over well in the arena of *public opinion*.

COA #2: THE "WE ARE REALLY GOING TO GET SERIOUS NOW!" OPTION

Advantages**:** The *cost* of this option appears acceptable because the real costs transfer to the backs of the states and their taxpayers. The *manpower* requirements of this option are acceptable because an additional 10,000 to 18,000 Border Patrol officers does not seem to be too extensive an enlargement of government in the name of border security. These increases in manpower translate to more civilian jobs and would tend to stimulate economies around the areas in which units are employed.

The stage of *public opinion* may also accept this option because at first blush it appears that we are really getting serious as we deploy more Border Patrol and National Guard assets to the border. Putting National Guard units on the border makes for a great sound bite in the media, but the reality is that they are only to serve in a supporting role. In other words, it briefs well but does not do much else.

Disadvantages: *Unity of command* and *unity of effort* are reasonably facilitated. However, ongoing counter-drug and counter-human-trafficking operations will not receive the maximum benefit from the synergistic opportunities afforded by common leadership and centralized command and control that's responsible for the orchestration of all operations connected to organized crime threats along our border and the countries and regions from which transnational organized crime originates.

This option does not maximize the *efficient use of resources* for much the same reason. In addition, as long as we continue to have to respond to the actions of the criminals and detain offenders once they are already in our country, we do not maximize the efficient use of our resources.

We do not maximize the potential synergistic effects of our *instruments of national power* under this approach. Through our *informational instrument,* we continue to try to soften the blow to our neighboring countries and the international community by stating that we are only placing more Border Patrol officers on our border, as we do not want to militarize our borders. At the same time, our government attempts to publicize this approach as a "get tough" policy to remedy the illegal activities that are running rampant in and around our border with Mexico.

We continue along the path of attempting to lift up underdeveloped and undeveloped countries through the use of our e*conomic instrument* in the forms of economic aid, trade agreements (NAFTA, CAFTA, CAFTA-DR) and direct infrastructure building. There is what appears as free acceptance of the assistance, but there is no meaningful change in many of the countries we are attempting to help.

This option relies on continued use of our d*iplomatic instrument* in such a way as to try to bring these other nations around to be more cooperative with the U.S. This is not a results-oriented tactic; it is action directed more at making people feel good about themselves than toward a substantive approach for real change and improvement.

Our *military instrument* is certainly not used to its full potential in this option and continues to be relegated to the role of playing "footsies" with our neighbors, so we can all feel good. The *effect on the U.S. economy* may be somewhat positive, but this option does not fully address the problem of the relatively free movement of illegal immigrants and drugs across our border. With it, we realize some restriction of illegal activities, but the criminals continue to find "soft spots" to exploit and our law enforcement agencies continue to be in reaction mode rather than forcing the enemy to react to us.

This course of action no doubt upsets the international community for all sorts of irrational reasons, but we should expect that any meaningful U.S. initiative to stem the tide of transnational criminal activities that originate from south of our border will meet with negative *international opinion.*

COA #3: THE "DECISIVE ACTION" OPTION

Advantages: Initially, the *cost* of this option appears to be significant, such as an estimated $2 billion for a barrier along the entire length of our border with Mexico. But we benefit from a long-term windfall of savings in other areas of our economy. For example, the states more than offset this federal expenditure with reduced demand on many state services, which potentially saves taxpayers in Texas alone an estimated $6 billion a year. In addition, crimes and internal enforcement of our drug laws decline because of drastically reduced entry of illicit drugs into America. The internal enforcement of the equation dramatically declines because potential violators are kept from ever entering the U.S. Due to this, state, local, and tribal law enforcement agencies are free to return to the duties and responsibilities for which they are most needed, instead of having to do the federal government's job. In truth, the list of cost savings could be much longer.

Unity of command and *unity of effort* are positive in this option because there is a clearly defined mission and resources given to the commander, SOUTHCOM, that would enable him to defend our border (and the surrounding air- and sea-lanes) and simultaneously conduct operations, as necessary, throughout Mexico, Central America, South America and the Caribbean. This approach maximizes the potential for fully integrated operations that can exploit the weaknesses of our adversaries in all dimensions.

This option facilitates the *efficient use of resources* in that the majority of counter-threat operations would be the responsibility of one commander. It is arguable that even though the military is part of the government, the military is a better steward of taxpayer dollars than the rest of the government. The state, local and tribal authorities would be able to concentrate on their traditional roles of law enforcement.

Under this COA, the U.S. maximizes the coordinated use of its *instruments of national power*. This option requires that the U.S. employ its *diplomatic instrument* in such a way as to make the affected countries realize that we mean business and that they can either become part of the solution or be treated as part of the problem. Mexico must understand that we are not going to allow them to exploit our country any longer, and if they fail to take appropriate steps to rectify conditions in their country that facilitate criminal enterprises in ours, we will take action to rectify the situation ourselves.

In this COA we use our *informational instrument* to educate Americans and the rest of the world about the severe threats arrayed against us and the reasons why we must act in our own national interest—because to do otherwise would mean the eventual end of the last promise of hope in the world. We employ our *economic instrument* using a "tough love" approach. Under this option, the U.S. ensures that the appropriate countries respond to our desires lest we withhold certain economic incentives.

This option sees our *military instrument* becoming fully integrated with the other instruments to yield an efficient foreign policy approach that will decisively curtail the wanton and flagrant disregard of U.S. sovereignty and human rights that is being perpetrated by many countries in our hemisphere. *Manpower* may appear to be a concern at first, but the military has forces available to accomplish this very important task for America and her people. If need be, the Congress should make an adjustment to end-strength that would enable America to defend herself. Moreover, once the border barriers are in place, the number of soldiers required will decrease.

The *effect on the U.S. economy* will be gradual. As sources of illegal income begin to dry up, certain sectors of the economy—banking, law enforcement, dining, services, etc.—will have to make adjustments due to decreased business. However, as the country realizes increased levels of wealth in both the private and public sectors, there will be a resultant expansion of economic growth.

Public opinion will overwhelmingly support this option because it sets a course that will get our border back under American control, and the result will be a corresponding reduction in all other threats facing America because of an open border.

Disadvantages: *International opinion* will probably resist it aggressively. Countries that exploit America are making huge profits, and they will not want to do without them. Corrupt governments will align themselves with a leftist, international media to try to shame America out of her get-tough policy. The affected countries will ignite additional international outrage because they will have to do something about their abysmal economies, governmental corruption and inadequate social services—and actually take care of business back home. They will no longer have the United States as a crutch.

So we have three COAs laid out before us. Now, because it is vital in determining which course of action to pursue, the military planners must immediately begin comparing them to identify the optimum recommendation to their commander. This is a critical aspect of the analysis as it facilitates the identification of the most optimum COA.

COMPARISON OF COA #1 AND COA #2

Both of these options appear to have *cost* savings at the federal level but continue to perpetuate transference of many associated costs to the states and localities. Option one has the edge in manpower at the federal level. Both options grossly lack provision for both *unity of command* and *unity of effort*; however, option two has a slight advantage over option one in that it does facilitate a higher degree of unity of effort by adding manpower to the border patrol.

Option two has the edge over option one in *efficient use of resources* because it reduces the instances of continued illegal activity in the southwestern United States. In addition, increases in *unity of command* and *effort* will provide more efficiency in the use of available resources.

Option one, more than option two, conserves *manpower*; option two increases it. Option two has a more positive *effect on the U.S. economy* than option one. Option two decreases the demands on social-service systems in the states, leaving state, local and tribal law enforcement better postured to carry out their primary law-enforcement tasks instead of having to augment federal enforcement initiatives.

The *instruments of national power* are not maximized in either option. The only substantive difference between the two options is an increase in Border Patrol officers with no change to the *status quo* regarding employment of our *informational, economic, diplomatic* and *military instruments of national power*. Option two would fare better than option one in *public opinion* because there is at least the appearance that the president is "getting serious" and doing something to counter the onslaught of illegal activities that are threatening our country.

In the realm of *international opinion,* option one would play better than option two because of the appearance of action in option two. Without applying any weights to the decision criteria, option two is better than option one by a margin of five to three, with one criterion (*instruments of national power*) being too close to call.

COMPARISON OF COA #1 AND COA #3

At the federal level, at least initially, the *costs* of option one are less than those of option three; however, much of the savings for the federal government mean costs that are transferred to the states and localities—and those are extremely high under option one as opposed to option three. In addition, the long-term costs would be much less in option three than in option one.

Option three has a much higher degree of *unity of command* and *unity of effort* than option one. At present, many agencies are cooperating but have neither clearly defined lines of command nor clearly defined duties and responsibilities, and these deficiencies tend to lead toward a lack of unity of effort. Contrast this to the clearly defined lines of command that are inherent in a military organization and the propensity for an efficient unity of effort. In light of these considerations, option three is more optimal than option one.

Consequently, option three would bear out a more *efficient use of resources* as opposed to option one primarily because of the consolidation of duties and responsibilities under the commander, SOUTHCOM, that should facilitate decisive operations throughout the depth of the threat organizations we are facing. In addition, by properly defending our southwestern border we would stymie many of the other threats because of their lack of ability to cross our border and affect the United States.

The *manpower* requirements for option one are less than they are for option three, but there are many state, local and tribal law enforcement agencies trying to compensate for the lack of action by the federal government. Again, it appears that there would be manpower savings for the federal government only. When we contrast this with option three, greater manpower requirements are placed on the federal government in the form of military forces (land, sea and air) needed to defend our southwestern border and conduct operations to counter the pervasive, ongoing illegal activities in the Western Hemisphere. Federal, state, local and tribal authorities will realize manpower savings as they will no longer have to chase after the bad guys once our border with Mexico is defended properly.

Option three will have a much more positive *effect on the U.S. economy* than option one because there will be greater opportunities for Americans to build wealth through reduced taxation (the illegals will not drain state and local services, the illicit-drug criminals will lose demand, etc.). Businesses will also experience financial benefits and opportunities to expand and grow. Of course, some sectors of the economy will have to adjust away from the financial benefits they are now receiving because of all the illegal activity resulting from an open border with Mexico.

Under option one, our *instruments of national power* are not fully integrated into a plan that will overcome the threats that we are facing. As long as our *informational, diplomatic, economic* and *military instruments* are used to pacify those concerned, there will be no significant progress to counter the many threats to our country. Conversely, in option three the intent is to synchronize all of our instruments of national power to achieve decisive results in the war on terror, the war on illicit drugs, the invasion of the United States by illegal immigrants and the fight against disease that is brought into our country by these offenders.

I predict that option three will receive support and backing from the American people and that option one will not be well received; therefore, option three will receive the greatest accolades in the arena of *public opinion*. A get-tough policy, as outlined in option three, will come under fire from the mainstream media and leftist politicians in this country, who will attempt to fan the flames of adverse *international opinion* against America and the majority of its citizenry who want our borders secured. Without applying any weights to the decision criteria, option three is better than option one by a margin of eight to one.

COMPARISON OF COA #2 AND COA #3

Option two has greater *cost* savings than option three. However, when we factor in the long-term cost savings, option three is the more optimal option. In addition, the cost savings of the federal government come at the expense of state, local and tribal systems that must pay much money out in services, education, health care, welfare, etc. because of inaction on the part of the federal government.

Option three has a much higher degree of *unity of command* and *unity of effort* than option two. At present, many agencies are cooperating but there are neither clearly defined lines of command nor clearly defined duties and responsibilities, and these deficiencies tend to lead toward a lack of unity of effort. The addition of more Border Patrol officers would add to unity of effort of the Border Patrol, but not necessarily to the many other agencies contributing to the overall effort to counter the threats facing the United States. Contrast this to the clearly defined lines of command that are inherent in a military organization and the propensity for an efficient unity of effort. In light of these considerations, option three is more optimal than option two.

Thus, option three supports a more *efficient use of resources* as opposed to option two primarily because of the consolidation of duties and responsibilities under the commander, SOUTHCOM, that should facilitate decisive operations throughout the depth of the threat organizations we are facing. In addition, by defending our southwestern border many of the other threats would be stymied (terrorists, drug trafficking, illegal immigration and disease) because of their lack of ability to cross our border and affect the United States.

The *manpower* requirements of option two would appear to be less than for option three, but there are many state, local and tribal law enforcement agencies caught up in trying to compensate for the lack of action by the federal government. Again, it appears that there would be manpower savings for the federal government only. When we contrast this with option three there are greater manpower requirements placed on the federal government in the form of military forces (land, sea and air) needed to defend our southwestern border and conduct operations to counter the pervasive, ongoing illegal activities in the Western Hemisphere. Federal, state, local and tribal authorities will probably realize manpower savings as they will no longer have to chase after the bad guys once our border with Mexico is defended properly.

Option three will have a more positive *effect on the U.S. economy* than option two. Gaining control of our southwestern border and taking the initiative against drug traffickers and illegal immigrants will reduce taxes for Americans. It will also better posture us to build wealth, and businesses will experience financial benefits and opportunities to expand and grow. Some sectors of the economy will have to adjust away from the financial benefits they are currently receiving from the illegal activity resulting from an open border.

Under Option 2 our *instruments of national power* are not fully integrated into a plan that will overcome the threats we are facing. As long as our *informational, diplomatic, economic* and *military instruments* are used to pacify those concerned, then there will be no significant progress to counter the many threats to our country. Conversely, in option three the intent is to synchronize all of our instruments of national power to achieve decisive results in the war on terror, the war on illicit drugs, the invasion of the United States by illegal immigrants and so on.

Consequently, I predict that option three will receive support and backing from the American people and that option two will be received less enthusiastically in comparison. Therefore, option three would receive the greatest accolades in the arena of *public opinion.* A get-tough policy, as outlined in option three, will come under fire from the mainstream media and leftist politicians in this country as they attempt to fan the flames of adverse *international opinion* against America and the majority of its citizenry who want our borders secured. Without applying any weights to the decision criteria, option three is better than option two by a margin of eight to one.

Based on the preceding analysis, COA #3 is the most favorable option. However, some criteria are more important than others. Therefore, each criterion receives a weight based on its relative importance in relation to the other criteria. For example, public opinion is much more important than international opinion, so public opinion receives a weight of five and international opinion receives a weight of one.

In the decision matrix, each criterion receives the number one, two or three based on the previous analysis. In each area of analysis the optimum COA receives a three and the least favorable COA receives a one. Then, each criterion's number is multiplied by that criterion's assigned weight to determine its subtotal. Finally, the subtotals are added and then compared. The COA with the greatest total is the most favorable.

The planners present the results of their analysis in the form of a decision matrix (Figure 3). The matrix is a concise, graphical portrayal of the critical information that makes it easier for the commander to make his decision.

Decision Matrix

Decision Criteria	COA#1	COA#2	COA#3
Cost (2)	2(2) = 4	1(2) = 2	3(2) = 6
Unity of Command (4)	1(4) = 4	2(4) = 8	3(4) = 12
Unity of Effort (4)	1(4) = 4	2(4) = 8	3(4) = 12
Efficient Use of Resources (4)	1(4) = 4	2(4) = 8	3(4) = 12
Manpower (2)	2(2) = 4	1(2) = 2	3(2) = 6
Effect on U.S. Economy (5)	1(5) = 5	2(5) = 10	3(5) = 15
Instruments of National Power (4)	1(4) = 4	1(4) = 4	3(4) = 12
Public Opinion (5)	1(5) = 5	2(5) = 10	3(5) = 15
International Opinion (1)	3(1) = 3	2(1) = 2	1(1) = 1
Totals	**37**	**54**	**91**

Figure 3

The decision, then, based on the analysis, is that the best course of action is COA #3. The United States should consider the implementation of a similar course of action. Once the commander, SOUTHCOM, approves such a course of action (step six of MDMP), his staff will carry out the remaining step—which is orders production.

Chapter Twenty-Four

A Path for the Future

Now that we've identified a potential COA for use by the federal government, let's get into more of the particulars associated with such a plan of action.

First, I propose that we assign the appropriate forces to the commander, SOUTHCOM, so he can control our southwestern border. The existing command and control structure—with some modifications to increase robustness—of the Department of Defense and SOUTHCOM have the capacity to expand the responsibilities of the cdr, SOUTHCOM. He is already responsible for certain operations that encompass most countries to the south of the United States in the Western Hemisphere.

In addition, to add some definition to the orders of magnitude that we may have to consider if we are to decisively defend our southwestern border, we should consider an initial deployment of a combat-ground force, in the neighborhood of 44,000 to 50,000 soldiers; this works out to about one infantry platoon per mile of frontage. This total is the number of combat soldiers needed on the border—infantry, armor (including cavalry) and field artillery. It does not include their combat support (CS) and combat service support (CSS) personnel totals. Moreover, this initial deployment figure does not include air, naval and Coast Guard personnel.

It makes sense to put the defenders of our border under SOUTHCOM because this command already coordinates and participates in activities with other countries to the south of the U.S. In addition, there are the counter-drug operations that SOUTHCOM supports and conducts in the war on drugs. Given all this, it's clear that the commander, SOUTHCOM, already has the situational awareness to carry out what needs to be done in the region. By giving him the responsibility of defense of the border, we will untie his hands and unify the effort and command as we have never before seen.

Just think of what this commander could accomplish if he were able to shut down the flood of illicit drugs across our border. Once this avenue is closed, he will be able to concentrate on the interdiction aspects of the war on drugs. This same logic applies to all of the other threats as well.

Since this will be a joint command there will be a need to package the force so as to counter threats in all dimensions, because this is not a two-dimensional war. Considering this fact, we have to dedicate assets that translate into the appropriate capabilities and that would posture those forces for success. If we fail to go at this endeavor with full measure, we will fail. We must be willing to put service biases and political correctness aside and move forward with the best plan possible. We cannot succumb to symbolism over substance in this most serious endeavor. Why? Because our citizenry deserves what the Constitution guarantees: defense of the homeland.

So what will our forces be looking at? The threat has air, land and sea assets and as we harden our southern border, the threats will increase their attempts to enter our country via air and sea.

Let me place the threat into proper context. Its land forces do not have an efficient, centralized and well-defined command and control structure. Nevertheless, as we begin to put pressure on them, they will respond with some innovations that may surprise us. What I mean by this is that we currently have several groups that are not necessarily operating in concert with each other, mainly because they are competing with each other for control of the illegal drug trafficking "rights" in the United States. But even when dealing with enemy combatants—and that's what these people are—they will more than likely find ways to cooperate with the other transnational criminal organizations because cooperation would be to their mutual advantage. That is just a consideration to watch because it will probably materialize and cause some modifications to how we are conducting our operations.

Another aspect of the enemy is that they are not merely ragtag misfits. We could refer to them as paramilitary forces, but, of course, many of them are capable *military* forces. Some of these Mexican-based, drug cartel, military forces were even trained by our own military before they took jobs with the bad guys.

Another aspect of our opposition that is well worth mentioning is that these illicit forces are not caring and compassionate about humanity, as are our military personnel. They are ruthless and extremely vicious. This is understandable when you consider the criminal activities they are in—for example, guns, prostitution and drugs.

The threat also has air and sea assets primarily used for transport. Given these enemy capabilities, that means that we have to be willing to tailor our forces to meet those threats. The commander, SOUTHCOM, will require additional naval and air assets. And, since the U.S. Coast Guard (USCG) is well-trained in counter-drug and counter-illegal-immigrant operations, it will have to provide expertise to the Navy when we employ those forces in support of U.S. SOUTHCOM.

The good news is that SOUTHCOM already has the pipelines in place to facilitate its expanded mission and to do what will be required. Some examples of current SOUTHCOM capabilities are:

1. Joint Interagency Task Force South (JIATF), which is responsible for conducting counter-illicit-drug-trafficking operations and partners with other countries in the region to accomplish this task.[178]
2. Joint Task Force-Bravo (JTF-B), which facilitates training in the area of Honduras.
3. Special Operations Command, South (SOC, South)
4. Additional naval department and air forces.

We will have to modify very little of the command and control and support structures that already exist within SOUTHCOM to enable it to take on the additional task of our nation's border defense.

The major change for SOUTHCOM will be increases in assets and capabilities in the military departments to enable the command to accomplish the mission. However, the military infrastructure is in place, and their situational awareness is superb.

The actual plan for implementation will be left up to the president, the secretary of defense (SECDEF) and the appropriate joint-level military planners. What I propose is at least a measure of the orders of magnitude we must consider if we are to adequately defend the homeland.

The bottom line is that the military can be deployed to and in place on the border in a matter of a few weeks, and can have the border controlled in very short order. I am confident, given the professionalism of our armed forces, that they will conduct themselves appropriately. There will be a learning curve and some growing pains—negligible at best—and then operations will smooth out and be extremely effective and efficient. Add to this the desert and near-desert terrain of much of the border areas, and we even have an ideal scenario to keep our troops combat-ready for Middle East operations in the global war on terror.

I am going to go out on a limb here and say that many people who live in close proximity to the border would enthusiastically welcome the military as liberators—I am absolutely sure of it.

Chapter Twenty-Five

Adjustments Within the U.S. Armed Forces

I will base my next discussion on two primary assumptions: 1) the global war on terrorism will continue for an undetermined number of years, and 2) the defense of our nation's borders is essential to the survival of the United States. In light of these two assumptions, we have another significant matter to address and that is our current force-mix of active duty, National Guard and reserve forces.

Our nation's military missions continue to increase, but we have not made any significant adjustments to our armed forces to meet these evolving commitments. It appears that we continue to ask our Armed Forces to "do more with less." This has been the norm for the last several years and is nothing new. How long can we realistically ask our military to keep doing more and more with less and less?

There may be naysayers from several quarters, but that is okay. My intent is to assist the American people in understanding how serious our situation actually is and to provide them a potential benchmark from which to decide what their elected politicians should be doing for them.

One concern that continues to arise pertains to the fact that our military appears to be stretched out very thin, and I can appreciate that argument. Nevertheless, there are some options open to the Congress. One is to address the respective end-strengths of the military departments. There is a move in

Congress to address this issue with proposed increases to the troop levels for ground forces, "including 30,000 to Army and 5,000 to Marine Corps active duty end-strength, and 17,000 Army National Guard end-strength."[179]

End-strength increases are needed, but are the proposed increases appropriate? Consider first that our present force-mix and the proposed end-strength increases are based on our current commitments and associated, ongoing military operations around the world. The proposed increases do not include the consideration of projected manpower needs based on an expanded military mission set to defend our nation's borders.

Increases in manpower are definitely needed and congressional initiatives that address this issue are steps in the proper direction. Nonetheless, I am not sure that the proposed increases are the best decisions, and here are some reasons why.

First, our force-mix is predicated on our current, ongoing operations and does little, if anything, to address our border defense manpower needs.

Second, the National Guard is currently operating in a more active-duty force role than a National Guard force role—at least in the traditional sense. The National Guard has been undertaking more and more of a dynamic role in the defense of our nation. However, the question is, should we expect our National Guard to continue deployments as if it were just another active duty force?

It would appear that their ongoing commitments, which will continue for the foreseeable future, are somewhat beyond their intended role as a part of our total force. Moreover, having National Guard forces on active duty is detrimental to the individual states that need them in reserve for natural disasters, civil unrest, etc. Additionally, those who sign up for duty in the National Guard typically are not planning to leave their families, lives and jobs for active duty—except in a *bona fide* emergency. Thus, the DOD is creating unnecessary hardships for these people and their families when it continues to rely on them as an active-duty force.

Third, assuming that we are expecting too much from the National Guard, is it necessary to increase the end-strength of the Army National Guard? From all that I have shared above, I must conclude in the negative.

We should be considering end-strength increases that are in keeping with the roles and missions of the military service departments. The primary mission-set of the active Army is to fight and win America's wars and defend her and the Constitution against all enemies both foreign and domestic. The National Guard plays a role in this as a member of the total force, but we should not expect the National Guard to be another active-duty force.

This brings me to a discussion of what our force-mix may more appropriately need to be. The emphasis should be on a significant increase in the active Army's end-strength and possibly the active Marine Corps' end-strength. After all, our current and projected requirements rely heavily on full-time ground-combat forces. Therefore, at minimum, I recommend that we consider reducing the Army National Guard's end-strength and increasing the active Army's end-strength.

In addition to adjustments in end-strengths, there is yet another option: adjustments to base-stationing plans. Why do we still have several units stationed in Western Europe? Against what threats are they defending? It appears that our government is more concerned with using scarce military resources to affect foreign relations and diplomatic policy. Apparently, our government thinks it is building relationships with other countries by having certain units forward deployed. I conclude that it is time to take a serious look at what we gain in diplomatic relations compared to what we are sacrificing in terms of not using these forces for the missions for which they are intended.

As our abilities to project forces both regionally and globally keep increasing, the need for forward-deployed units decreases. And don't forget to factor in that there are enormous costs associated with maintaining all of these forces overseas and that in bringing them home there will be a significant cost savings.

Another option is to consider stationing some of the units in the U.S. to positions that are closer to where they are needed. Some examples are the units at Fort Carson, Colorado; Fort Drum, New York; Fort Lewis, Washington; Fort Riley, Kansas; and Fort Stewart, Georgia. Obviously, for this program to succeed, congressmen from those states, which may experience a reduction in military forces as they are deployed to more-needed areas of the country, would have to place our nation's defense as a priority over their own political agendas.

My point is that we have the forces available right now for what we need accomplished, but are we willing to use them for the purpose for which they were designed—to defend our nation? Or are we going to continue to use them for other political reasons and leave everything as it is?

In summary, I continue to hear, with regard to our United States Army and Marine forces, first that our active duty forces are stretched to the limit, if not beyond and second that our National Guard forces are being relied upon to too great a degree and their deployments are beyond that which was originally intended for their use. Third, the argument given regarding the National Guard also applies to our reserve forces—who are equally over-deployed.

If these concerns are true reflections of reality, then Congress and the DOD should consider making the appropriate adjustments to the end-strengths of our active-duty, National Guard and reserve forces. It appears that the answer to the critical needs of our nation would dictate that we reduce our reliance on our National Guard and reserve forces and rely more on our active-duty forces—especially domestically, rather than sending them forward, deployed in places where there is no longer a need.

There are some similar concerns that pertain to the United States Navy (USN) and the United States Coast Guard (USCG), but they are not exactly the same as those that face the Army and Marine Corps. Our first consideration is the fact that the USCG is the lead federal agency for maritime homeland security. A second consideration is that the USCG has both homeland security missions and non-homeland security missions.

According to a Congressional Research Service Report for Congress,[180] there are real concerns that the USCG is not able to perform all of its missions. At present, the USCG is expected to perform five homeland security missions: "(1) ports, waterways, and coastal security, (2) drug interdiction, (3) migrant interdiction, (4) defense readiness, and (5) other law enforcement."[181]

The missions of the USN and USCG are, respectively, fighting America's wars at sea and law enforcement, but I propose that we realign them. First, we should consider that since we are in a war in our hemisphere, the USN should be responsible for mission sets that are associated with national defense. Second, given my plan of action, it would be appropriate to realign drug and immigrant interdiction under the USN, who would dedicate forces to work under SOUTHCOM. The USCG would then support the USN in these areas, rather than being the lead force.

Third, to an extent yet to be determined between the DOD and the DHS, there would have to be a clear delineation of duties and responsibilities between USN and USCG forces as they defend the nation as part of SOUTHCOM, and the USCG duties and responsibilities in support of law enforcement operations as a part of homeland security. At minimum, certain USCG assets would have to be task-organized to support the JFMCC, SOUTHCOM.

It is worthy to note that the USCG excludes drug interdiction and other law enforcement from its definition in its FY2007 budget submission to Congress. It appears that the USCG excluded these roles because they are not able to accomplish them.

Aside from the military, we should consider taking maximum advantage of contract support (civilian, private enterprise support) of our border duty forces.

There are four primary areas wherein we can make good use of contract services: logistics support, base camp construction and maintenance, detention facility construction and operations, and barrier placement.

Once the joint planners complete SOUTHCOM's campaign plan, they will know where they need base camps, detention facilities, operating bases and so on. Then, once the requirements contracts are ready to go, it will be up to the DOD contracting agencies to compete and award the appropriate contracts. The DOD has significant experience in this area because of operations in Afghanistan and Iraq, as well as in other areas around the world, including the United States.

Since we are talking about contracting, I want to put on the inspector general hat that I used to wear in the Army and strongly recommend that we tailor a quality assurance (QA) and inspection program to monitor and periodically inspect the contract services provided to the military forces in support of border defense operations. Many of you are aware of the waste, fraud and mismanagement of taxpayer dollars by certain private contractors that have supported our forces in Afghanistan and Iraq. I propose a no-nonsense QA program that would safeguard against the typical unethical behavior of many private contractors when they are working for the government.

I recommend that whatever we do in the area of QA, we consider using personnel from the Army's Inspector General Corps. These men and women are impartial keepers of standards, and I am confident that they can monitor and ensure compliance of contract services to our border forces.

Chapter Twenty-Six

Congressional Inaction on Border Defense

As we conclude this section, it would be beneficial to compare the congressional solutions we discussed earlier with the one presented in this section. Without question, there are stark differences to note.

If you read some of the House and Senate versions you would see numerous references to "studies" and "assessments" before making any final decisions regarding meaningful immigration reform and control. This means more wasted time, increased growth in the number of government employees, and more committees and study groups—who typically decide that another meeting is required in order to decide what to do.

Reading House resolution H.R.4437 and Senate bill S.2611, it is obvious that there is basically no common ground between the two. This baffles me. How can the House put together a bill that is consistent with the desires of the majority of Americans while the Senate puts together a bill that doesn't even come close to what Americans want?

In December 2005, the House passed H.R.4437 (Border Protection, Antiterrorism, and Illegal Immigration Control Act of 2005) by a 239–182 or fifty-seven percent margin. The provisions of H.R.4437 "would strengthen border and immigration controls, including deployment of a fence and surveillance equipment along the Mexico-U.S. border."[182]

In contrast, the Senate version (S.2611) has provisions that are merely political rhetoric. It calls for amnesty by effect, though not by name, no significant hardening of the U.S.-Mexico border, a guest worker program, a path to citizenship for all illegal immigrants (with some exceptions), emphasis on internal enforcement—and it raises the numbers for legal immigration to the United States. Does this make sense to anyone? Surely, not to U.S. citizens and legal immigrants.

Both of the above bills, especially S.2611, call for all kinds of increases in spending as well as the hiring of more government employees, cooperation between departments and so on. In addition, there are numerous references to "cooperation" between various government agencies and the Department of Defense with regard to the many capabilities that DOD possesses. Apparently, the House and the Senate believe that the DOD capabilities should be shared with DHS, at minimum, and that these assets could be put to good use in securing our border.

They are correct that these assets would be ideal for border defense—but give me a break here. The Department of Homeland Security is already 180,000 employees strong. The House and Senate plans both call for increases in manpower in several areas of the DHS over the next few years—and I predict that the DHS will easily be over 200,000 strong in a very short time. The respective bills also call for $1.2 billion here, still more billions there, $50 million for this, more millions for that, and the list goes on. Some of the spending allotments include:

- *Establishing a committee* called the Center of Excellence for Border Security. This means hiring more government employees and funding their salaries—paid for by the taxpayers.
- *Having the inspector general (IG), DHS review all contracts in excess of $20 million.* I have personal and intimate experience with this approach, and all it does is cause the contractors to submit bids that are below the $20 million threshold. Some strategies to get around this include splitting contracts that are actually part of the same requirement—for example, submitting two contracts for $10 million apiece instead of just one for $20 million—or

submitting a bid for just under the $20 million threshold when the contractor's actual cost is much less.

- *Establish an Office of Air and Marine Operations.*
- *Establish an office for intelligence coordination and sharing, as relates to the southwestern border, between DHS and...who?*

Can you guess how many of the 180,000 DHS employees are on our borders? As of 2004, there were fewer than 2,000 agents on the Mexican and Canadian borders at any given time.[183] This is another example of an already bloated government bureaucracy, so top heavy that it can barely get out of its own way. Now Congress wants to expand it more? That is simply more government waste—with very little fixed responsibility on those within its system.

Now, many of the agents on the ground are doing great work, and they are not the ones about whom I speak. I am referring to many of the government civilians who comprise the monolithic bureaucracy of the Department of Homeland Security. We need more agents on the ground, not more recipients of "welfare with honor" within the bureaucratic chain.

We have the military units available now, and all we have to do is direct their employment where we need them most and place them under the command of the commander, SOUTHCOM. If we did, the border would be properly defended in no time. Why duplicate the assets we already have in the military? Worse yet, why put those military assets under the control of civilian bureaucrats or law enforcement personnel who have no idea how to use them properly?

Let the Border Patrol and the USCG concentrate on ports of entry and other related matters—they are trained for that. Allow state, local and tribal law enforcement agencies to perform their traditional roles. With the military on the border we will not have to rely on cooperation to the extent outlined in current legislative proposals for immigration reform and enforcement. Cooperation is inherently inefficient and costly—and good only for political expediency. Do we want to solve the border problem or not?

As we harden a fixed system of barriers along our southern border, we can also begin to reduce the number of military forces required to accomplish the mission of defending that border. Thus, our efficiency increases as time goes on using the COA I propose, and assets will be reassigned later as needed. This is a significant departure from the politicians' proposals to build new government institutions that will likely last for eternity.

As we close this section, let me share with you some questions that we need to ask ourselves. My excessive use of the word "expert" below may seem quite redundant—but I assure you that this is intentional. I want to emphasize this point because I firmly believe that the answers to these questions may help to settle your mind on the issue of whether we should use our military on the U.S.-Mexico border. Consider:

- Who are the experts in counterinsurgency operations?
- Who are the experts in reconnaissance and surveillance operations?
- Who are the experts in desert operations and operations on all other types of terrain, for that matter?
- Who are the experts in putting together a comprehensive plan that will defend our southern border?
- Who are the experts at determining the best barriers that will be needed to accomplish border defense?
- Who are the experts in detention center operations?
- Who has the medical personnel embedded in its organization to render medical aid?
- Who has personnel with the appropriate language skills?
- Who are the experts in interaction with foreign citizens?
- Who are the experts in conducting combat operations in response to an armed military force that tries to force a border crossing in support of drug trafficking and other armed transnational criminal activities?
- Who has the assets needed to maneuver in all dimensions (land, air, sea and space) to defend our border with Mexico?
- Who has reliable inspectors general embedded in their organization?
- Of all the branches, agencies, offices, etc. within the U.S.

government, which is the most efficient and conscientious steward of taxpayer dollars?
- Who has the ability to expeditiously integrate replacements into its forces and carry on continued operations in a seamless manner?
- Which forces are far less likely to be corrupted by the criminal forces that try to corrupt America with bribes, extortion and such?
- Which government organization does not have to worry about overtime pay?
- Who are the experts in the tactical operations to defend our country?
- Who has the responsibility to defend this nation against all enemies foreign and domestic and uphold the Constitution of the United States?
- Who has the discipline, principles, ideals, values, etc., to accomplish any mission?

I could go on and on, but the answer to all of the above questions is the United States armed forces. Thus, let's push our elected representatives to make the quality decisions necessary to secure our country—efficiently, effectively and expeditiously—using our U.S. military.

Conclusion

Do we still have options, both as a people and as a nation? The answer is an overwhelming "yes." This is not the time for Americans to stack arms and give up. One of my intentions in this endeavor is to shine a light on some of the problems facing America so that people will be aware of the gravity of our situation.

Our Constitution is an extraordinary document that places specific limits on the powers that the states delegate to the federal government. This is the true fount of our rule of law. If we were to hold the government accountable for its violations of this rule, many of the problems that we are witnessing today would disappear. With this in mind, we as individuals and we as states should exercise the powers that we retained when our forefathers voluntarily entered into our contract with the federal government.

We can seek change in some areas through the elective and legislative processes. However, there are adjustments that we can effectuate in *each* of the branches of government that could go a long way toward returning the power to the people and removing it from the government—in essence, moving from ruler's law to people's law.

The first adjustment would take place in the executive branch, which currently has the power of executive order—a usurpation of legislative authority—but does not have the real power of veto. Only the legislative branch has the constitutional authority to pass laws and appropriate money, and the president's use of the executive order violates this check of the legislative over the executive.

The executive branch's inability to effectively veto aspects of proposed legislation that cause it to be laden with unrelated amendments—often separate and distinct acts within a single bill—is a violation of the presentation clauses and the executive's veto authority. We should either require that all legislation presented to the executive be focused on one objective or issue at a time, or we should allow the executive the line-item veto. The inability of the executive to effectively veto legislation violates the president's check on the legislative branch.

The second adjustment involves the legislative branch, which is out of control. It's true that the Founders intended to vest the legislative branch with the sole power of the purse; however, this authority has been perverted by Congress. It is important to understand that congressmen are not federal representatives; rather they are representatives *to* the federal government. The Congress is composed of delegations from the states, and those delegations represent the interests of their constituents, which, in turn, leads to the representation of each state's interest.

The problem, then, is that Congress has too much power due to its unfettered ability to tax and redistribute money. Three potential remedies could assist in rectifying this situation. First would be to require Congress to adhere to the constitutional requirement that it cannot take an individual's property, in this case an individual's money, and give it to another. Our current tax system provides the means by which Congress pursues its ends, which are to control almost every aspect of our lives and to buy votes that serve to perpetuate the representatives in their positions of supposed power.

Ask yourself why the states continue to throw good money after bad while the federal government refuses to act on so many problems of concern to the citizens of this great country. Many aspects of current federal policy stymie the states in their pursuit of ensuring the rights and liberties of their citizens. Often, the federal government keeps us under control through its funding programs to the states.

So, why don't the states throw off this yoke and stand as the sovereigns the Founders intended they be? Why do the states give revenue to the federal government only to receive, after the government takes its processing fee, in many cases, a pittance in return, along with all the strings that come with that money?

In an effort to remove the means that Congress uses to maintain control, we should require that Congress maintain a balanced budget and call for the repeal of the Sixteenth Amendment—the second possible remedy to Congress' overabundance of power. The Founders intended that there be checks on the federal government by the state governments; the Sixteenth Amendment effectively removes one of those checks, and so it needs to go.

The third possible remedy would be enacting appropriate state-level laws to ban political contributions that do not come from individuals. (This is not a federal matter because the states are responsible for their own elections.) It is arguable that the domination of big money in politics is the root cause of governmental corruption of the law of the land but personally, I do not believe that there should be limits on what individual citizens decide to give to candidates. Such contributions are a way for them to have their desires known and they should be allowed to offer up as much as they want to. However, I do believe that we should consider only allowing contributions from individuals who live within the district in which an election is taking place.

An example could be a congressional race wherein only the registered voters from a particular district would be eligible to exercise an aspect of their right of free speech in the election. No contributions from political action committees, government, unions, associations or any other special interest groups should be allowed. As it stands now, many of these groups influence elections in areas where they do not reside. Why should they have the opportunity to influence other people's elections? Voters from within the district should be the only ones influencing their elections.

In the end, it's really all about money, because money means power. We have to get some checks in place to control congressional spending. The rule of law manifested in our Constitution is supposed to be the check, but Congress disregards the rule of law as prescribed by the Founders.

Another option would be for states to interject themselves again into the process of collection and remittance of federal taxes. The states should consider what burdens they incur because of the federal government's inaction when it comes to its constitutional charter to defend the nation and in response, not remit the monies they spend on doing the government's job. An example is the money that the states spend because the federal government refuses to do anything substantive about our southern border.

This problem—the federal government's neglect of its duties—could be an offshoot of the dynamic of the few controlling the many, which I mentioned earlier. One solution to this problem could be found in term limits, which the Founders referred to as "rotation" during the constitutional debates. Term limits seem to be a viable way to break the paradigm of business as usual in Washington as well as at the state and local levels. The Twenty-second Amendment places term limits on the office of the president of the United States, and some states already have term limits on their politicians but I think it can still go further. A universal standard of two terms for senators and four for congressmen would potentially serve to invigorate government rather than perpetuate career politicians who act like landed gentry rather than responding to the will of the people.

Contributors to this mentality include congressional salaries and entitlement programs. After a few years in Congress many representatives and senators are literally rich. With this in mind, the states should consider taking control of their delegations' salaries. I would consider it wise to remove our representatives from the federal payroll and place them on the payrolls of their own states, with states deciding just what their salaries should be.

As it is now, however, the Constitution provides, in Article I, Section 6, that "a compensation"[184] be paid to representatives in the Congress by the federal treasury. If this is to stand, then the federal compensation they get should be no more than reimbursement for travel to and from legislative sessions and a *per diem* based on itemized cost-of-living expenses while the members are away from their homes. Any and all entitlement programs for which congressmen are eligible should be transferred to the states, which can decide whether to participate or not. In addition, I recommend that we do away with congressional retirements and healthcare benefits altogether.

In short, I believe that politicians should not receive financial enrichment for what is supposed to be selfless service. They should get in, do their duty, and return home.

In another area of the government, the judicial branch is not upholding its end of the constitutional contract with the people of this country either. The courts must adhere to the rule of law as intended by the Founders, which means that they must only consider the law when developing their opinions. When the judiciary oversteps its constitutional bounds and sets social policy, it is usurping the authority that was invested solely in the state legislatures. In such a case, the executive branch should not enforce the court's opinion, and the legislative branch should consider removing jurisdiction on the matter that was abused by the court.

To begin with, when selecting candidates for the Supreme Court of the United States, the executive and legislative branches of government must use a litmus test that entails asking specific questions about certain aspects of the Constitution. An example could be a question about whether or not the Second Amendment forbids the federal government from infringing in any way on the right of a citizen to keep and bear arms on his or her person. If the candidate answers "yes," then that person would be eligible for continued consideration to serve on the court; however, an answer in the negative would disqualify that person from further consideration.

There *is* right and wrong in the words of our Constitution, and we should be selecting judges that understand the rule of law as it was originally intended by the Founders.

In summary, in order to secure our nation, I believe that we must:

1. Defend our border with Mexico. As a part of that defense, we must be willing to go all the way and make maximum use of the United States armed forces.
2. Place regular military forces on the borders, including land, air and sea, to defend our nation against the threats that are facing us and will continue to face us.
3. Place all military border defense forces under the direct combatant command of the commander, Southern Command, with appropriate federal agencies in support, to allow him the capability to conduct operations to defend our great nation.
4. Establish, as appropriate, temporary detention centers that meet the needs for which intended and nothing more.

5. Enforce our existing internal immigration laws.
6. Shift law enforcement's priorities to internal enforcement and enforcement at ports of entry, and use criminal profiling techniques as appropriate.
7. Mandate that English be the official language of the United States.
8. Stop educating illegal immigrants in our schools. If the courts get involved, the legislature should enact the appropriate exception to remove the jurisdiction from the courts.
9. Stop allowing illegal immigrants access to our social services except for well-defined cases that require emergency care. If the courts get involved, the legislature should enact the appropriate exception to remove the jurisdiction from the courts.
10. Stop abusing the Fourteenth Amendment, and send illegal immigrants back to their countries of origin as soon as possible; if this involves an infant this means as soon as it is able to travel. If the courts get involved, the legislature should enact the appropriate exception to remove the jurisdiction of such cases from the courts.
11. Return illegal immigrants who enter from or through Mexico back to Mexico, regardless of their countries of origin.
12. Consider moratoriums on the legal immigration of Islamics, Hispanics and Latinos to the United States.
13. Repeal the Seventeenth Amendment and return the election of U.S. senators to the state legislatures.
14. Prohibit sanctuary policies.
15. Designate Mexico as ineligible for aid because of its continued failure to meet the requirements of our international drug control certification.
16. Designate countries that do not fully comply with the minimum standards for the elimination of slave trafficking as tier three, and, therefore, designate them as ineligible for any and all forms of foreign aid.
17. Designate Mexico as a tier three trafficking in persons country

and deny it, and all other tier three countries any and all foreign aid.

18. Add a third element to the federal anti-drug initiative that requires that our border with Mexico be sealed.
19. Implement a comprehensive and well regulated health-screening program for all potential immigrants to the U.S. Deny all potential immigrants who fail their health screenings to immigrate to the United States. Do not accept any immigrants with unhealthy, preexisting medical conditions.
20. Modify the *Posse Comitatus* Act to facilitate military operations in defense of our border with Mexico if necessary.
21. Not enter into a Social Security totalization agreement with Mexico.
22. Pass legislation that prohibits U.S. businesses from accepting the *matricula consular* card as personal identification.
23. Pass legislation that penalizes U.S. businesses for practices that support illegal immigrant fraud and/or asset acquisition.
24. Enforce existing laws against businesses that knowingly hire illegal immigrants.
25. Remove all other incentives that encourage illegal immigrants to enter or stay within the United States.
26. End the policy of chain migration.
27. Be willing, on the state level, to do that which is necessary to preserve the rights and liberties of our people if the federal government continues to do nothing in defense of our nation.

Is there a light at the end of the tunnel for America? Absolutely, but only if we as a nation are willing to face reality, jettison political correctness and get down to the business required to ensure the continued success of the great experiment that is the United States of America. After all, we are truly the greatest nation on God's earth. Without the leadership of the United States the rest of the world will never advance into a prosperous future, only move toward decline and decay. Furthermore, we must do what is necessary before it is too late.

Appendix I

Joint Statement[185]

Joint Statement
Security and Prosperity Partnership of North America
Issued: March 23, 2005 from Waco, Texas
by President Bush, President Fox, and Prime Minister Martin

We, the elected leaders of Canada, Mexico, and the United States, gather in Texas to announce the establishment of the Security and Prosperity Partnership of North America.

Over the past decade, our three nations have taken important steps to expand economic opportunity for our people and to create the most vibrant and dynamic trade relationship in the world. Since September 11, 2001, we have also taken significant new steps to address the threat of terrorism and to enhance the security of our people.

But more needs to be done. In a rapidly changing world, we must develop new avenues of cooperation that would make our open societies safer and more secure, our businesses more competitive, and our economies more resilient.

Our Partnership would accomplish these objectives through a trilateral effort to increase the security, prosperity, and quality of life of our citizens. This work would be based on the principle that our security and prosperity are mutually dependent and complementary, and would reflect our shared belief in freedom, economic opportunity, and strong democratic values and institutions. Also, it would help consolidate our action into a North American framework to confront security and economic challenges, and promote the full potential of our people, addressing disparities and increasing opportunities for all.

Our Partnership is committed to reach the highest results to advance the security and well-being of our people. The Partnership is trilateral in concept; while allowing any two countries to move forward on an issue, it would create a path for the third to join later.

ADVANCING OUR COMMON SECURITY

We would establish a common approach to security to protect North America from external threats, prevent and respond to threats within North America, and further streamline the secure and efficient movement of legitimate, low-risk traffic across our shared borders. As part of our efforts, we would:

- Implement common border security and bioprotection strategies;
- Enhance critical infrastructure protection, and implement a common approach to emergency response;
- Implement improvements in aviation and maritime security, combat transnational threats, and enhance intelligence partnerships; and
- Implement a border facilitation strategy to build capacity and improve the legitimate flow of people and cargo at our shared borders.

ADVANCING OUR COMMON PROSPERITY

We would work to enhance North American competitiveness and improve the quality of life of our people. Among other things, we would:

- Improve productivity through regulatory cooperation to generate growth, while maintaining high standards for health and safety;
- Promote sectoral collaboration in energy, transportation, financial services, technology, and other areas to facilitate business; and invest in our people;
- Reduce the costs of trade through the efficient movement of goods and people; and
- Enhance the stewardship of our environment, create a safer and more reliable food supply while facilitating agricultural trade, and protect our people from disease.

NEXT STEPS

We would establish Ministerial-led working groups that would consult with stakeholders in our respective countries. These working groups would respond to the priorities of our people and our businesses, and would set specific, measurable, and achievable goals. They would identify concrete steps that our governments can take to meet these goals, and set implementation dates that would permit a rolling harvest of accomplishments.

Within 90 days, Ministers would report back to us with their initial report. Following this, the groups would report on a semi-annual basis. Because the Partnership would be an ongoing process of cooperation, new items would be added to the work agenda by mutual agreement as circumstances warrant.

Through this Partnership, we would ensure that North America remains the most economically dynamic region of the world and a secure home for our people in this and future generations.

Appendix II

Corrupt Governments

- **Aruba**: transit point for U.S.-bound narcotics with some accompanying money-laundering activity.
- **The Bahamas**: transshipment point for cocaine and marijuana bound for U.S.; offshore financial center.
- **Barbados**: one of many Caribbean transshipment points for narcotics bound for the U.S.; offshore financial center means potential for money-laundering operations.
- **Belize**: transshipment point for cocaine; small-scale illicit producer of cannabis (includes hashish and marijuana) for the international drug trade; money-laundering activity related to narcotics trafficking and offshore sector.
- **Brazil**: illicit producer of cannabis; important transshipment country for Bolivian, Colombian and Peruvian cocaine headed for Europe; also used by traffickers as a way station for narcotics air transshipments between Peru and Colombia; upsurge in drug-related violence and weapons smuggling; important market for Colombian, Bolivian and Peruvian cocaine; illicit narcotics proceeds earned in Brazil are often laundered through the financial system.

- **British Virgin Islands**: transshipment point for South American narcotics destined for the U.S.; large, offshore financial center makes it vulnerable to money laundering.
- **Colombia**: illicit producer of coca (the plant source of cocaine), opium poppy and cannabis; world's leading coca cultivator; the world's largest producer of coca derivatives; supplying most of the U.S. market and the great majority of cocaine to other international drug markets; important supplier of heroin to the U.S. market; a significant portion of non-U.S. narcotics proceeds are either laundered or invested in Colombia through the black market peso exchange; major corruption is still a problem. (Note: Do you have any idea how much money and manpower we have in and continue to dedicate to this country in the war on drugs? A well-orchestrated counter-drug operation is an absolute must or we will never make any substantive headway in the war on drugs.)
- **Costa Rica**: transshipment country for cocaine and heroin from South America; domestic cocaine consumption, particularly crack cocaine, is rising.
- **Dominican Republic**: transshipment point for South American drugs destined for the U.S.; has become a transshipment point for ecstasy from the Netherlands and Belgium destined for U.S.; substantial money-laundering activity; Colombian narcotics traffickers favor the Dominican Republic for illicit financial transactions.
- **Guyana**: transshipment point for narcotics from South America to the U.S.; producer of cannabis; rising money laundering related to drug trafficking and human smuggling.
- **Haiti**: Caribbean transshipment point for cocaine *en route* to the U.S.; substantial money-laundering activity; Colombian narcotics traffickers favor Haiti for illicit financial transactions; pervasive corruption. (Note: I thought we went in and saved this country already!)

- **Honduras**: transshipment point for drugs and narcotics; illicit producer of cannabis; corruption is a major problem; some money-laundering activity. (Note: Do you have any idea how much foreign aid we export to this nation? Our military has been in this country for many years, building infrastructure and performing nation-building operations. Based on the CIA's report, it appears that our efforts are really paying off—or maybe not.)
- **Jamaica**: transshipment point for cocaine from South America to North America and Europe; illicit cultivation of cannabis; corruption is a major concern; substantial money-laundering activity; Colombian narcotics traffickers favor Jamaica for illicit financial transactions.
- **Mexico**: major drug-producing nation; major supplier of heroin and largest foreign supplier of marijuana and methamphetamine to the U.S. market; continues as the primary transshipment country for U.S.-bound cocaine from South America, accounting for about ninety percent of estimated annual cocaine movement to the U.S.; major drug syndicates control majority of drug trafficking throughout the country; producer and distributor of ecstasy; significant money-laundering center. (Note: I find it interesting that we do not come out and call Mexico what it really is: extremely corrupt in many aspects of its society. How else can there be so much trafficking of illegal commodities from and through Mexico if the government is not corrupt? When I read through the information that the State Department provides, it did not mention the corruption that exists in Mexico either. I wonder if that is because Mexico is our "friend.")
- **Panama**: major cocaine transshipment point and primary money-laundering center for narcotics revenue; monitoring of financial transactions is improving (focus is prevention of drug-related money laundering); official corruption remains a major problem. (Note: I thought we

fixed all of these problems years ago when we invaded this corrupt country. I stand corrected.)

- **Venezuela**: illicit producer of opium and coca for the processing of opiates and coca derivatives; however, large quantities of cocaine, heroin and marijuana transit the country from Colombia bound for U.S.; significant narcotics-related money-laundering activity; increasing signs of drug-related activities by Colombian insurgents on border. In addition, this country is emerging as a terrorist hub in the Western Hemisphere, and is issuing identity documents that could be used to obtain a U.S. visa for entry into the U.S.[186]
- **United States**: world's largest consumer of cocaine, shipped from Colombia through Mexico and the Caribbean; consumer of heroin, marijuana and, increasingly, methamphetamine from Mexico; consumer of high-quality Southeast Asian heroin; illicit producer of cannabis, marijuana, depressants, stimulants, hallucinogens and methamphetamine; money-laundering center. (Note: It appears that we are just as guilty, if not more so, than many countries that benefit from our neglect to do what is right and proper for our citizens. Make no mistake: We are definitely a major source of our own problems. What a shame.)

Note: The primary source for the preceding information, except where otherwise noted, is the CIA's *The World Factbook 2008*.[187]

Selected Bibliography

I found enormous amounts of information during the course of my research in preparation for this project. I have tried in earnest to cite all sources of information that I used. One realization that I want to mention is that there are many of us who are like-minded, and it is apparent that when those of us of a certain mindset analyze relevant data, we often arrive at similar conclusions and recommendations. In this limited bibliography, my intent is to provide some examples of readings I have done that have influenced my opinions, conclusions and recommendations.

The Anti-Federalist Papers and the Constitutional Debates, edited by Ralph Ketchum, A Signet Classic, New York, NY, 1986.

The Federalist Papers, by Alexander Hamilton, James Madison, and John Jay, edited by Gary Willis, Bantam Books, New York, NY, 1982.

The Making of America: The Substance and Meaning of the Constitution, by W. Cleon Skousen, National Center for Constitutional Studies, third edition, revised, 2007.

The American Constitutional Order: History, Cases, and Philosophy, Douglas W. Kmiec, Stephen B. Presser, John C. Eastman, and Raymond B. Marcin, LexisNexis, 2004.

Applied Economics: Thinking Past Stage One, Thomas Sowell, Basic Books, New York, NY, 2004.

The Basic Works of Aristotle, edited by Richard McKeon, The Modern Library, New York, NY, 2001.

The Bill of Rights, Akhil Reed Amar, Yale University Press, New Haven and London, Connecticut, 1998.

Black's Law Dictionary, Bryan A. Garner Editor in Chief, West Publishing Company, Saint Paul, MN, 2001.

Cicero de Republica de Legibus, translated by C.W. Keyes, The Loeb Classical Library, Cambridge, MA, 2000.

Coercing Virtue: The Worldwide Rule of Judges, Robert H. Bork, The American Enterprise Institute, Washington, D.C., 2003.

The Common Law, Oliver Wendell Holmes, Jr., Dover Publications, Inc., New York, NY, 1991.

The Constitution in Exile, Judge Andrew P. Napolitano, Nelson Current, Nashville, TN, 2006.

Constitutional Chaos, Judge Andrew P. Napolitano, Nelson Current, Nashville, TN, 2004.

Constitutional Law National Power and Federalism: Examples and Explanations, Christopher N. May and Allan Ides, Aspen Publishers, New York, NY, 2004.

The 5000 Year Leap: Principles of Freedom 101, by W. Cleon Skousen, National Center for Constitutional Studies, 2006.

The Forgotten Man: A New History of the Great Depression, Amity Shlaes, Harper Publishers, New York, NY, 2007.

Goldwater, Barry M. Goldwater with Jack Casserly, Doubleday, New York, NY, 1988.

Great Dialogues of Plato, translated by W.H.D. Rouse, A Signet Classic, New York, NY, 1999.

Men in Black: How the Supreme Court is Destroying America, Mark Levin, Regnery, Washington, D.C., 2005.

In Mortal Danger: The Battle for America's Border and Security, Tom Tancredo, World Net Daily Books, Nashville, TN, 2006.

To Renew America, Newt Gingrich, Harper Collins, New York, NY, 1995.

Slouching Towards Gomorrah, Robert H. Bork, Regan Books, New York, NY, 2003.

So Help Me God, Roy Moore, B&H Publishers, Nashville, TN, 2005.

The Tempting of America, Robert H. Bork, Touchstone, New York, NY, 1991.

The Way Things Ought to Be, Rush Limbaugh, Pocket Books, New York, NY, 1992.

Winning the Future, Newt Gingrich, Regnery Publishing, Inc., Washington, D.C., 2005.

Achtung-Panzer!, Major-General Heinz Guderian, translated by Christopher Duffy, Arms and Armor, New York, NY, 1992.

The Alamo and Texas War for Independence, Albert A. Nofi, Combined Books, Conshohocken, PA, 1992.

The Art of War, Sun Tzu, translated by Samuel B. Griffith, Oxford University Press, New York, NY, 1971.

The Art of War in the Western World, Archer Jones, University of Illinois Press, Chicago, IL, 1987.

A Critical Analysis of the Gulf War, Colonel Harry C. Summers, Jr. (Ret.), A Dell Book, New York, NY, 1992.

Field Manual 100-5 Operations, the War Department, United States Government Printing Office, Washington, D.C., 1941.

Field Manual 100-5 Operations, Headquarters, Department of the Army, Washington, D.C., 1993.

Field Manual 100-15 Corps Operations, Headquarters, Department of the Army, Washington, D.C., 1996.

Field Manual 101-5 Staff Organization and Operations, Headquarters, Department of the Army, Washington, D.C., 1997.

A General's Life, Omar N. Bradley, Simon and Schuster, New York, NY, 1983.

Joint Doctrine Capstone and Keystone Primer, General John M. Shalikashvili, Chairman, Joint Chiefs of Staff, Washington, D.C., 1997.

Joint Publication 3-09 Doctrine for Joint Fire Support, Vice Admiral Dennis C. Blair, Director, Joint Staff, Washington, D.C., 1998.

Lost Victories, Field Marshall Erich von Manstein, translated by Anthony G. Powell, Presidio, Novato, CA, 1982.

Maneuver Warfare Handbook, William S. Lind, Westview Press, Boulder, CO, 1985.

Memoirs of General William T. Sherman, Da Capo Press, New York, NY, 1984.

Memoirs of Robert E. Lee, A.L. Long, The Blue and Gray Press, Secaucus, NJ, 1983.

Mighty Stonewall, Frank E. Vandiver, Texas A&M University Press, New York, NY, 1957.

On Strategy, Colonel Harry C. Summers, Jr. (Ret.), A Dell Book, New York, NY, 1984.

On War, Carl von Clausewitz, translated by Michael Howard and Peter Paret, Princeton University Press, 1976.

The Patton Papers: 1940-1945, Martin Blumenson, Houghton Mifflin Company, Boston, MA, 1974.

Patton's Principles, Porter B. Williamson, Touchstone, New York, NY, 1979.

Personal Memoirs of U.S. Grant, General U.S. Grant, Da Capo Press, New York, NY, 1982.

The Rommel Papers, Field Marshall Irwin Rommel, edited by B.H. Liddel-Hart, translated by Paul Findlay, Da Capo Press, New York, NY, 1953.

Soldat: Reflections of a German Soldier, 1936-1949, Siegfried Knappe and Ted Brusaw, Orion Books, New York, NY, 1992.

Soviet AirLand Battle Tactics, William P. Baxter, Presidio Press, Novato, CA, 1986.

19 Stars, Edgar F. Puryear, Jr., Presidio, Novato, CA, 1971.

Theodore Rex, Edmund Morris, Random House, New York, NY, 2001.

War as I Knew It, General George S. Patton, Jr., Houghton Mifflin Company, Boston, MA, 1947.

Endnotes

1 Congressman Steve King, "The Pence immigration plan—the wrong kind of proposal at the worst possible time," U.S. Border Control, http://www.usbc.org/opinion/2006/summer/penceplan.htm.
2 The Majority Staff of the House Committee on Homeland Security, Subcommittee on Investigations, "A Line in the Sand: Confronting the Threat at the Southwest Border," The United States House of Representatives, http://www.house.gov/mccaul/pdf/Investigaions-Border-Report.pdf.
3 Douglas Farah, "Russian Mob, Drug Cartels Joining Forces," *Washington Post*, September 29, 1997.
4 ABC News staff, "Run Silent, Run Drugs: The Cocaine Sub Fleet," ABC News, http://blogs.abcnews.com/theblotter/2007/12/run-silent-run.html.
5 Personal interview with a Costa Rican national in December 2006.
6 Central Intelligence Agency, *The World Factbook*, Central Intelligence Agency, https://www.cia.gov/library/publications/the-world-factbook/geos/mx.html.
7 Ibid.
8 Ibid.
9 Jane Blackmore, "U.S.-Mexico Border on Brink of Full Blown War," *Newsmax*, August 2008, 20-21.
10 Washingtonpost.com staff, "Iraq War Casualties," *The Washington Post*, http://www.washingtonpost.com/wp-dyn/content/article/2008/08/30/AR2008083002057.html.
11 The National Institute on Drug Abuse staff, "Magnitude," National Institutes of Health National Institute on Drug Abuse, http://www.nida.nih.gov/about/welcome/ aboutdrugabuse/magnitude/.

12 International Drug Trade and U.S. Foreign Policy, Congressional Research Service—The Library of Congress, July 21, 2006, CRS-2.
13 International Drug Trade and U.S. Foreign Policy, CRS-7.
14 International Drug Trade and U.S. Foreign Policy, CRS-8.
15 International Drug Trade and U.S. Foreign Policy, CRS-4.
16 Kevin Mooney, "Texas Sheriffs Say Terrorists Entering U.S. from Mexico," CNSNews.com, http://www.adjunct.diodon349.com/Attack_on_USA/texas_sheriffs_say_terrorists_entering_US_from_Mexico.htm.
17 Ibid.
18 Beth Gorham, "Latest U.S. Terror Case Similar to Canada's 'Homegrown' Busts," *Canadian Press*, June 24, 2006.
19 Dr. Cosman, Ph.D., "Illegal Aliens and American Medicine," *Journal of American Physicians and Surgeons* 10 (Spring 2005), 8.
20 Ibid.
21 Ibid.
22 Ibid.
23 Ibid.
24 Bill Murphy, "County's cost for illegal immigrants' care soars/Radack: Burden of federal policy shouldn't fall on the local taxpayer," *Houston Chronicle*, June 17, 2006.
25 Kevin Bales, Laurel Fletcher and Eric Stover, "The Hidden Slaves: Forced Labor in the United States" (California: Human Rights Center, University of California, Berkley, 2004), 35.
26 EA Talbot, M Moore, E McCray, NJ Binkin, "Tuberculosis among foreign-born persons in the United States, 1993-1998" *Journal of the American Medical Association* (December 2000), 894-900.
27 Ibid.
28 Eileen Schneider, Kayla F. Laserson, Charles D. Wells, Marisa Moore, "Tuberculosis along the United States-Mexico border, 1993-2001," *Revista Panamericana de Salud Pública* 16 (July 2004).
29 Ibid.
30 Ibid.
31 WHO.int staff, "Emergence of XDR-TB," World Health Organization, www.who.int/mediacentre/news/notes/2006/np23/en/index.html.
32 United States Department of Homeland Security, *Yearbook of Immigration Statistics: 2007* (Washington, D.C.: U.S. Department of Homeland Security, Office of Immigration Statistics, 2008), 91-92.
33 *Plyler v. Doe*, 457 U.S. 202 (1982).
34 The Majority Staff of the House Committee on Homeland Security, Subcommittee on Investigations, "A Line in the Sand."

35 Brad Knickerbocker, "Illegal immigrants in the US: How many are there?" *The Christian Science Monitor*, www.csmonitor.com/2006/0516/p01s02-ussc.html.

36 Ibid.

37 WorldNetDaily.com staff, "Illegals estimated to number 18-20 million," WorldNetDaily, http://www.worldnetdaily.com/news/article.asp?ARTICLE_ID= 42216.

38 Knickerbocker, "Illegal immigrants in the US."

39 Congressman Tom Tancredo, *In Mortal Danger: The Battle for America's Border and Security* (Nashville, TN: WorldNetDaily Books, 2006).

40 Bryan A. Garner, *Black's Law Dictionary*, Second Pocket Edition (West Group, 2001), 630.

41 BBC News staff, "France prepares new anti-riot law," BBC News, http://news.bbc.co.uk/1/hi/world/europe/6098458.stm.

42 Daily Times staff, "Get out if you want Sharia law, Australia tells Muslims," *Daily Times*, http://www.dailytimes.com.pk/default.asp?page=story_25-8-2005_pg1_2.

43 Alan Travis and Madeleine Bunting, "British Muslims want Islamic law and prayers at work," *Guardian*, http://www.guardian.co.uk/print/0,,5074487-115039,00.html.

44 Cnn.com staff, "Clinton Will Fight to the Finish; McCain Courts Democrats & Independents; Amnesty for Illegal Aliens; Border Boondoggle: Virtual Fence is Ineffective," CNN.com, http://transcripts.cnn.com/TRANSCRIPTS/0804/23/ldt.01.html.

45 Mark Leon Goldberg, "How International Organizations Combat Human Trafficking," UN Dispatch, http://www.undispatch.com/archives/2008/06/how_international_organizations_combat_human_trafficking.php.

46 Department of State staff, "Trafficking in Persons Report June 2007," Department of State, http://www.state.gov/documents/organization/82902.pdf.

47 United States Department of Justice Civil Rights Division, "Trafficking in Persons—A Guide for Non-Governmental Organizations," United States Department of Justice, http://www.usdoj.gov/crt/crim/wetf/traffickbrochure.html.

48 Ibid.

49 Clare Ribando Seelke, Alison Siskin, "CRS Report for Congress," U.S. Department of State, http://fpc.state.gov/documents/organization/109559.pdf.

50 Barnaba Institute staff, "What Does Barnaba Institute Do?" The Barnaba Institute, http://www.barnabainstitute.org/2.html.

51 Ibid.

52 Meredith May, "Sex Trafficking," *San Francisco Chronicle*, October 6, 2006.

53 United States Department of Justice Civil Rights Division, "Trafficking in Persons—A Guide for Non-Governmental Organizations."
54 Seelke, Siskin, "CRS Report for Congress."
55 May, "Sex Trafficking."
56 Human Rights Center, "Freedom Denied," Organization of American States, http://www.oas.org/atip/country%20specific/Forced%20Labor%20in%20California.pdf.
57 Ibid.
58 May, "Sex Trafficking."
59 Ibid.
60 Ibid.
61 Ibid.
62 U.S. Department of Justice Child Exploitation and Obscenity Section, "Child Prostitution," U.S. Department of Justice, http://www.usdoj.gov/criminal/ceos/prostitution.html.
63 Ibid.
64 ABCNews staff, "Teen Girls' Stories of Sex Trafficking in U.S.," ABCNews, http://abcnews.go.com/Primetime/story?id=1596778.
65 Ibid.
66 Charles M. Goolsby, Jr., "Dynamics of Prostitution and Sex Trafficking from Latin America into the United States," LibertadLatina.org, http://www.libertadlatina.org/LL_LatAm_US_Slavery_Report_01_2003.htm.
67 Ibid.
68 Ibid.
69 Zona Latina staff, "*Machismo* in Latin America," Zona Latina, http://www.zonalatina.com/Zldata77.htm.
70 LibertadLatina.org staff, "United States-Latina Sex Slavery," LibertadLatina.org, http://www.libertadlatina.org/US_Latina_Sex_Slavery.htm.
71 Pendra Lee Snyder, "Ohio identified as a hub for Human Trafficking," CitizenUSA, http://www.ccn-usa.net/news.php?id=492.
72 Humantrafficking.org staff, "Human Trafficking in Boston, USA," humantrafficking.org, http://www.humantrafficking.org/updates/515.
73 Hispanic Tips staff, "Prostitution sting nets 8 arrests so far in North Carolina," Hispanic Tips, http://www.hispanictips.com/2006/08/29/prostitution-sting-nets-arrests-north-carolina/.
74 The Associated Press, "25 indicted in alleged 'major prostitution ring,'" WinonaDailyNews.com, http://www.winonadailynews.com/articles/2007/05/22/mn/2min22.txt.
75 LibertadLatina.org staff, "String of Latino Brothels Found in Virginia and Maryland Suburbs [of Washington, DC]: Police Say Women Come from New York," Libertad

Latina.org, http://www.libertadlatina.org/US__LATINO%20BROTHELS_VA_MD_WOMEN_FROM_NEW%20YORK%20_09-21-1994.HTM.
76 Ibid.
77 LibertadLatina.org staff, "United States-Latina Sex Slavery."
78 Darla Miles, "'Slave trade' growth prompts action in FW," KVUE.com, http://www.kvue.com/news/state/stories/081707kvueslavetrade-eh.4247b468.html.
79 MySA staff, "Details emerge in human trafficking case in San Antonio," MySA, http://www.mysanantonio.com/news/MYSA060207_01A_human_trafficking_folo_35909ae_html12421.html.
80 United States Department of State, "Trafficking in Persons Report 2008 - Mexico," UNHCR, http://www.unhcr.org/refworld/docid/484f9a2cc.html.
81 U.S. Department of State, "Country Narrative-Mexico," Human Trafficking Website 2009, http://gvnet.com/humantrafficking/Mexico-2.htm.
82 Department of State staff, "Trafficking in Persons Report June 2007."
83 Ibid.
84 NationMaster.com staff, "Tier rating (most recent) by country," NationMaster.com, http://www.nationmaster.com/graph/cri_tra_iss_tra_in_per_tie_rat-issues-trafficking-persons-tier-rating.
85 Department of State staff, "Trafficking in Persons Report 2008," U.S. Department of State, http://www.state.gov/documents/organization/105658.pdf.
86 Ibid.
87 Ibid.
88 Ibid.
89 Judge Robert Bork, *The Tempting of America* (Free Press, 1989) 176.
90 Christopher N. May and Allan Ides, *Constitutional Law, Examples and Explanations* (Aspen Publishers, 2004), 37
91 Gary Wills, ed., *The Federalist Papers*, (Bantam Classic, 1982), 197.
92 Ibid., 193.
93 Ibid., 380.
94 Ibid., 460.
95 Ibid., 466.
96 Charles P. Cozic, ed., *Illegal Immigration Opposing Viewpoints* (San Diego: Greenhaven Press, Inc., 1997), 66.
97 Bork, *The Tempting of America*, 180-182.
98 Melissa Dodson and Erin McCann, "The Evaluation of Texas A&M University System's Support Activities Related to Limited English Proficient Student Success Initiative, Cycle I Grants, Final Report," Southwest Educational Development Laboratory, http://ritter.tea.state.tx.us/opge/progeval/LimitedEnglish/ExecSumm_04-06.pdf.
99 *Plyler v. Doe*, 457 U.S. 202 (1982).

100 Ibid.
101 Ibid.
102 Ibid.
103 Ibid.
104 Ibid.
105 Law.com staff, "*Posse comitatus*," Law.com Dictionary, http://dictionary.law.com/default2.asp?typed=posse+comitatus&type=1&submit1.x=68&submit1.y=18&submit1=Look+up.
106 Bryan A. Garner, ed., *Black's Law Dictionary, Second Pocket Edition* (St. Paul: West Group, 2001) 537.
107 Worldnetdaily.com staff, "Text of Bush's address on immigration," Worldnetdaily.com, http://www.worldnetdaily.com/news/article.asp?ARTICLE_ID=50223.
108 Wills, *The Federalist Papers*, 455.
109 Ibid., 214.
110 Garner, *Black's Law Dictionary*, 467.
111 Ibid., 329.
112 Will, *The Federalist Papers*, 228.
113 FoxNews.com staff, "Groups Decry Renegade Border Guards," FoxNews.com, http://www.foxnews.com/story/0,2933,152557,00.html.
114 Associated Press, "Powell says border walls won't work," Boston.com, http://www.boston.com/news/world/latinamerica/articles/2006/06/08/powell_says_border_walls_wont_work/.
115 Ibid.
116 Edwin Meese III, "An Amnesty by Any Other Name…" *The New York Times*, May 24, 2006, Washington Edition.
117 CNN.com staff, "Bush Addresses Nation on Immigration," CNN.com, http://transcripts.cnn.com/TRANSCRIPTS/0605/15/ng.01.html.
118 Ibid.
119 OnTheIssues staff, "Third Bush-Kerry Debate: on Immigration," OnTheIssues, http://www.ontheissues.org/Archive/Bush_Kerry_3_Immigration.htm.
120 Office of the Chief of Police, "Special Order No. 40," JudicialWatch, http://www.judicialwatch.org/archive/2006/so40-gates.pdf.
121 Dr. Kevin P. McNamee, DC, L.Ac., "Immigration—Legal and Illegal: United States, California, and Los Angeles," California Health Institute, http://www.californiahealthinstitute.com/CHI_immigration.pdf29 May 2006, 11.
122 Ibid., 26.
123 HB1804, Oklahoma Taxpayer and Citizen Protection Act of 2007.
124 Rhymes With Right staff, "Border Jumper Care Costs Harris County Taxpayers $97,300 Annually," Rhymes With Right, http://rhymeswithright.mu.nu/archives/182250.php.

125 Jeff Oliver, "States struggle to cut costs of immigration," *Christian Science Monitor*, June 21, 2006.
126 Congressman Gary Miller, quoted on http://fredfryinternational.blogspot.com/2007/05/mexico-and-us-governments-are.html.
127 CRS Report for Congress, *Mexico-U.S. Relations: Issues for the 109th Congress*, January 20, 2006, Congressional Research Service—The Library of Congress
128 Central Intelligence Agency, *The World Factbook*.
129 Iadb.org staff, "Who we are," Inter-American Development Bank, http://www.iadb.org/aboutus/whoWeAre.cfm?lang=en.
130 Inter-American Development Bank staff, "Inter-American Development Bank Annual Report 2005," Inter-American Development Bank, http://idbdocs.iadb.org/wsdocs/getdocument.aspx?docnum=705662.
131 Iadb.org staff, "Remittances to Latin America and the Caribbean 2007," Inter-American Development Bank, http://www.iadb.org/mif/remesas_map.cfm.
132 Ibid.
133 Multilateral Investment Fund, Inter-American Development Bank, "Remittances 2005: Transforming Labor Markets and Promoting Financial Democracy, Inter-American Development Bank, http://idbdocs.iadb.org/wsdocs/getdocument.aspx?docnum=639199.
134 Iadb.org staff, "Remittances to Latin America and the Caribbean 2007."
135 Ibid.
136 Ibid.
137 King, "The Pence immigration plan."
138 Ssa.gov staff, "U.S. International Social Security Agreements," SocialSecurityOnline, http://www.ssa.gov/international/agreements_overview.html.
139 CNN.com staff, "Lou Dobbs Tonight: The Debate Over Immigration & Border Security Continues," CNN.com, http://transcripts.cnn.com/TRANSCRIPTS/0604/01/ldt.01.html.
140 The Phyllis Schlafly Report staff, "Ripoff of American Workers and Taxpayers," *The Phyllis Schlafly Report*, Vol.39, No.10, May 2006.
141 Ana Radelat, "An Avalanche of Aid: Hispanic workers Flood the Gulf Coast," Hispanic Magazine, HispanicMagazine.com.
142 McNamee, "Immigration—Legal and Illegal," 16.
143 CNN.com staff, "Lou Dobbs Tonight: Encore Presentation: Broken Borders," CNN.com, http://premium.cnn.com/TRANSCRIPTS/0610/29/ldt.01.html.
144 Will, *The Federalist Papers*, 236.
145 Ibid., 237.
146 Ibid., 238.
147 Ibid., 238.
148 Ibid., 239.

149 Ibid., 237-239.
150 Tony Blankley, "Mexican illegals vs. American voters,"Townhall.com, http://townhall.com/columnists/TonyBlankley/2006/03/29/mexican_illegals_vs_american_voters.
151 S.2611 (Comprehensive Immigration Reform Act of 2006), 109th Congress, 2nd Session.
152 Ibid.
153 Ibid.
154 Steven A. Camarota, "Amnesty Under Hagel-Martinez: An Estimate of How Many Will Legalize If S. 2611 Becomes Law," Center for Immigration Studies, http://www.cis.org/articles/2006/back606.html.
155 Ibid.
156 H.R.6061 (Secure Fence Act of 2006), 110th Congress, 2nd Session.
157 Ibid.
158 Ibid.
159 Ibid.
160 Senate Bill Clerk, "U.S. Senate Roll Call Votes 109th Congress - 2nd Session," United States Senate, http://www.senate.gov/legislative/LIS/roll_call_lists/roll_call_vote_cfm.cfm?congress=109&session=2&vote=00262.
161 Spencer S. Hsu, "In border fence's path, legislative roadblocks," MSNBC, http://www.msnbc.msn.com/id/15149231/.
162 Ibid.
163 Ibid.
164 H.R.6094 (Community Protection Act of 2006), 109th Congress, 2nd Session.
165 H.R.6095 (Immigration Law Enforcement Act of 2006), 110th Congress, 2nd Session.
166 Cathy Lowne, *Speeches That Changed the World* (London: Bounty Books, 2006), 162.
167 Joint Publication 1-02, *Department of Defense Dictionary of Military and Associated Terms*, June 10, 1998, 428.
168 JP 1-02, 326.
169 JP 1-02, 443.
170 U.S. Department of Army, *Field Manual 101-5, Staff Organization and Operations*, May 31, 1997.
171 JP 1-02, 345.
172 JP 1-02, 163.
173 Carl von Clausewitz, *On War* (Princeton: Princeton University Press, 1976), 120.
174 JP 1-02, 239.
175 JP 1-02, 239.

176 FM 100-15, *Corps Operations*, Headquarters, Department of the Army, 29 October 1996.

177 United States. Department of Homeland Security. *Yearbook of Immigration Statistics: 2007*. Washington, D.C.:

U.S. Department of Homeland Security, Office of Immigration Statistics, 2008.

178 Southcom.mil staff, "Interagency," United States Southern Command Partnership for the Americas, http://www.southcom.mil/appssc/pages/interagency.php.

179 Stephen Daggett, "Defense: FY2007 Authorization and Appropriations," Federation of American Scientists, http://www.fas.org/sgp/crs/natsec/RL33405.pdf.

180 Ronald O'Rourke, "Homeland Security: Coast Guard Operations—Background and Issues for Congress," Federation of American Scientists, http://fas.org/sgp/crs/homesec/RS21125.pdf.

181 Ibid.

182 Mark P. Sullivan and June S. Beittel, "Mexico-U.S. Relations: Issues for the 109th Congress," Federation of American Scientists, http://fas.org/sgp/crs/row/RL32724.pdf.

183 Cis.org staff, "The High Cost of Cheap Labor: Illegal Immigration and the Federal Budget," Center for Immigration Studies, http://www.cis.org/articles/2004/fiscalexec.html.

184 Will, *The Federalist Papers*, 454.

185 Security and Prosperity Partnership of North America, "Leaders' Statement: Security and Prosperity Partnership of North America Established," Security and Prosperity Partnership of North America, http://www.spp-psp.gc.ca/progress/spp_established-en.aspx.

186 The Majority Staff of the House Committee on Homeland Security, Subcommittee on Investigations, "A Line in the Sand," 4.

187 Central Intelligence Agency, *The World Factbook*.